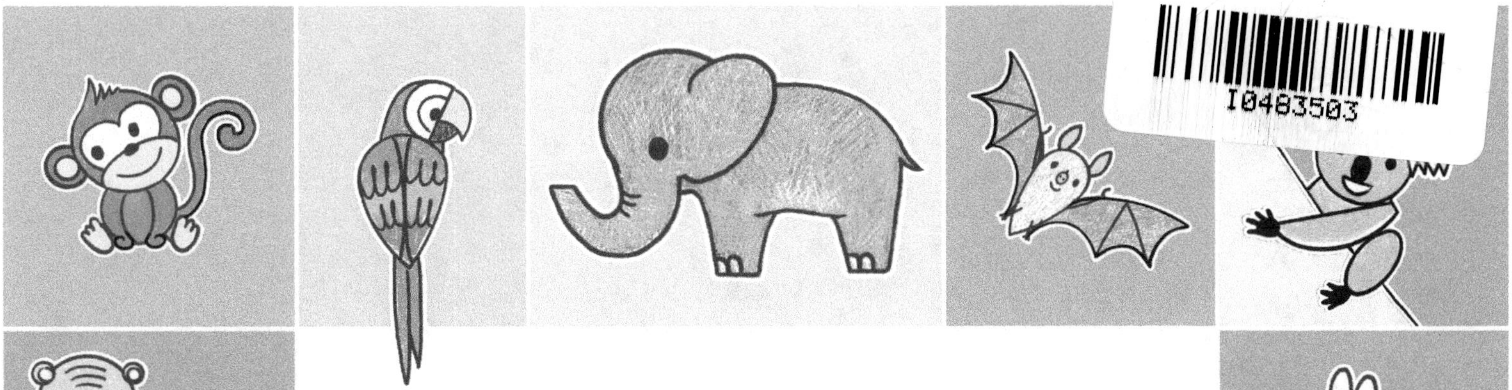

Draw & Learn™

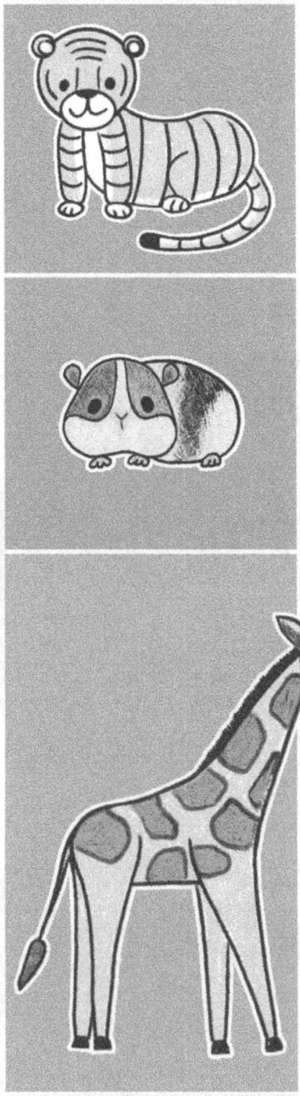

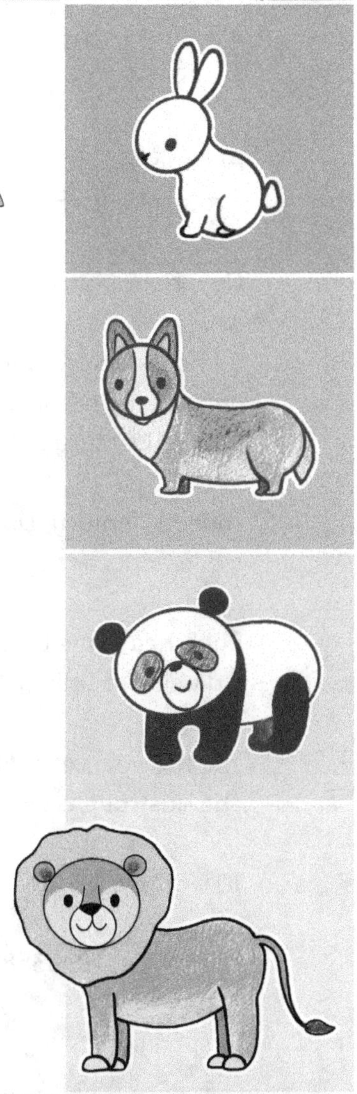

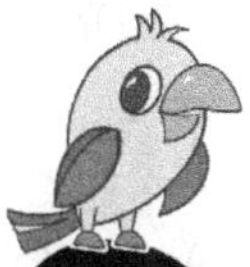

ANIMALS

a step-by-step drawing guide for kids

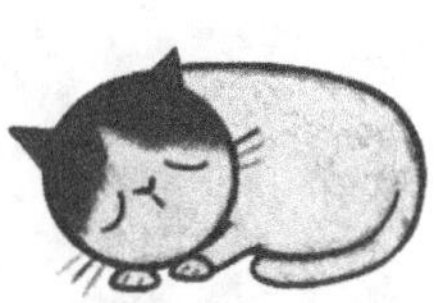

Draw & Learn Book Series

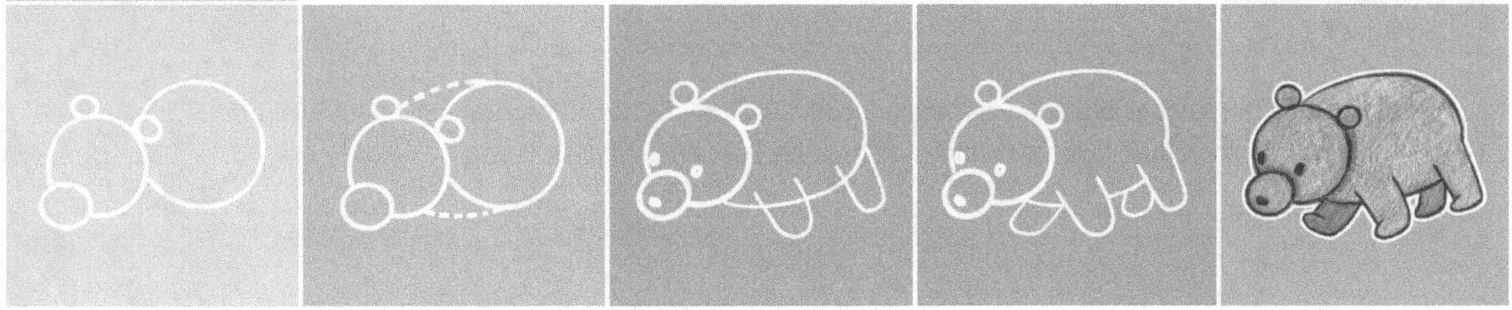

Alisa Bloom

Animals: A Step-by-Step Drawing Guide for Kids
Draw & Learn Book Series

Infinite Century, Draw & Learn, Artessi, Artessi+, Artessi Children's Books, and the colophon are trademarks or registered trademarks of Infinite Century LLC.

Published in the United States by Artessi Children's Books, an imprint of Infinite Century Publishing, a division of Infinite Century LLC.

The text was set in Artessi Pro, Century Kids, and Starbook.
The illustrations were created in mixed media: pencil and digital.

10 9 8 7 6 5 4 3 2 1

ISBN 978-0-9983582-7-7

First Edition

Ages 6+

Summary: This engaging guide from the educational Draw & Learn™ series inspires children to learn how to draw their favorite animals using simple lines and shapes.

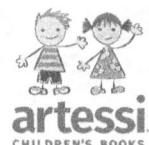

artessi
CHILDREN'S BOOKS

Discover Draw & Learn™ books, journals, and more at
www.artessi.com

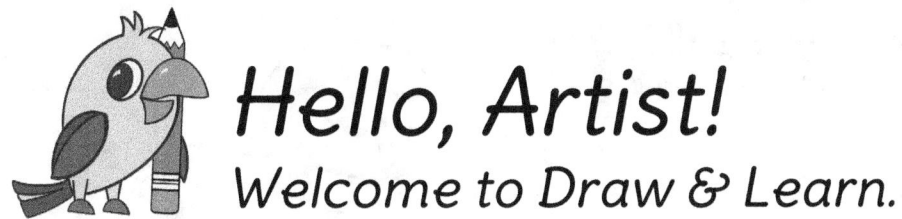

Hello, Artist!
Welcome to Draw & Learn.

Join Artie the Bird on a drawing adventure into the world of animals! Begin by practicing drawing simple lines, shapes, and patterns. Then, learn how to draw amazing animals and discover where they live, what they eat, and how they behave.

You'll explore lots of fun drawing activities and make a paper doll. At the back of this book, you'll find a special section just for you to sketch and write down your ideas. So grab your favorite crayons and pencils and let's get started. But first, write your name here:

This book belongs to

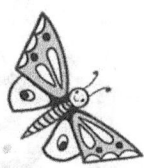

_____

Note to Grown-Ups

The *Draw & Learn* guides and activity books use visual art and fun science facts to foster creativity and imagination in children. With easy-to-follow steps, the drawing lessons in this exciting guide can be completed with little or no adult help. Even so, we encourage you to take time to enjoy reading, learning, and creating art together.

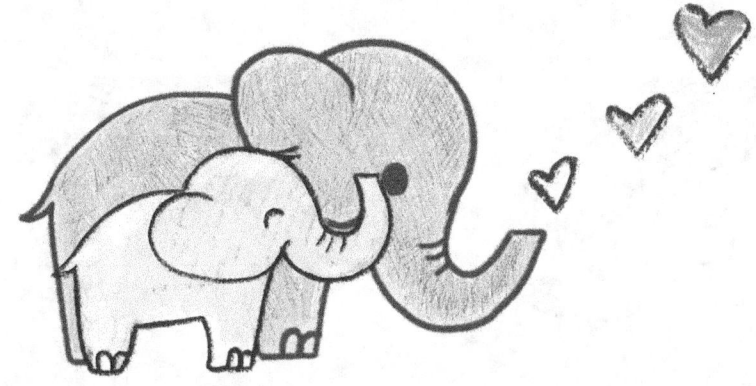

Book Map

Start here 7

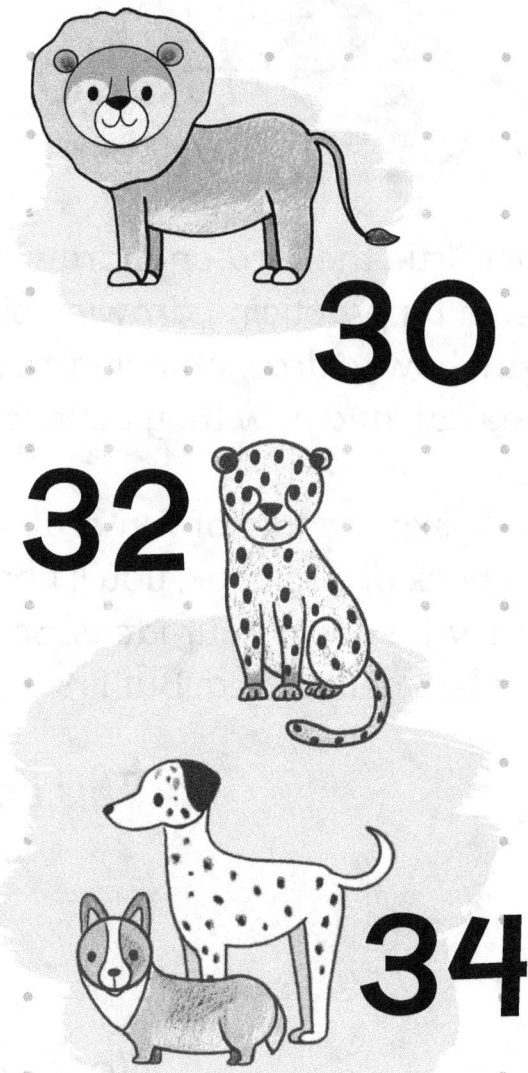

30

14

32

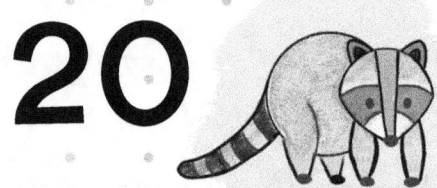 18

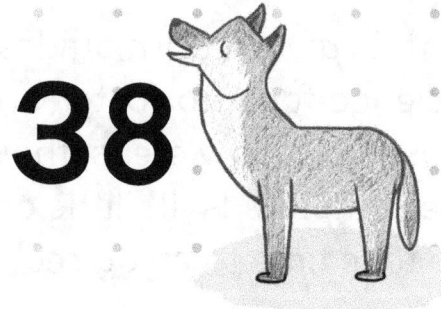

34

20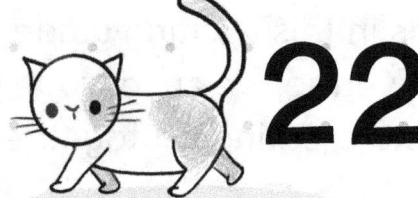

38

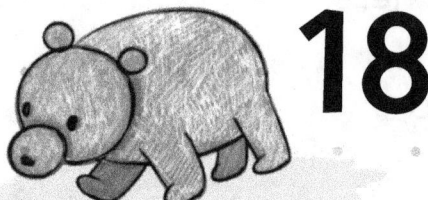 22

28

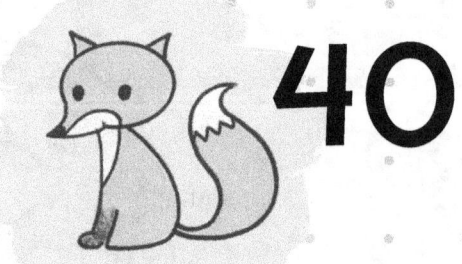 40

44

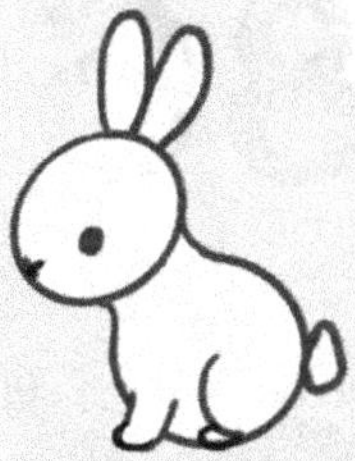

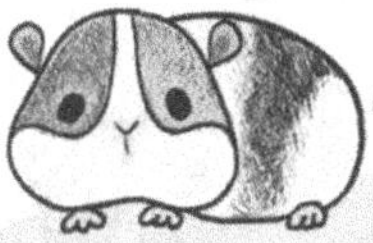

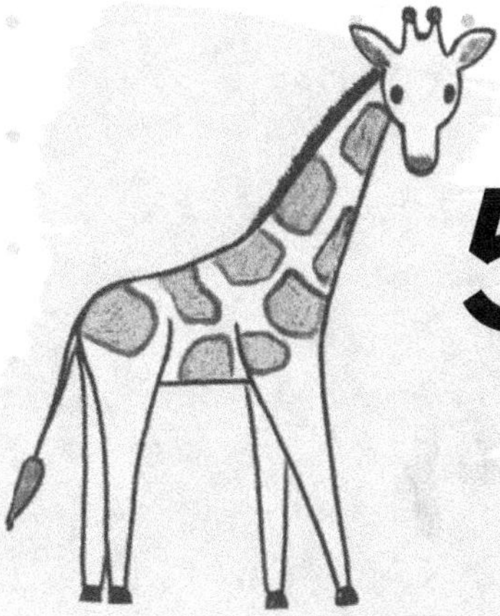

58

48

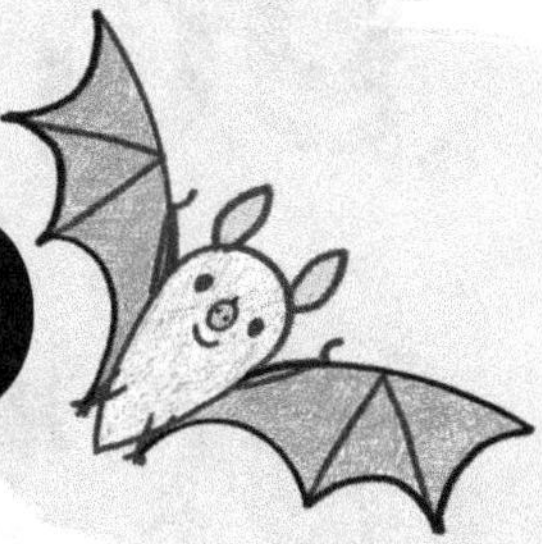

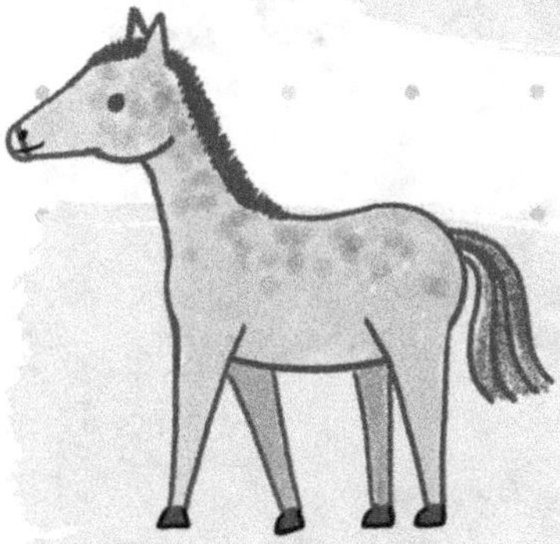

60

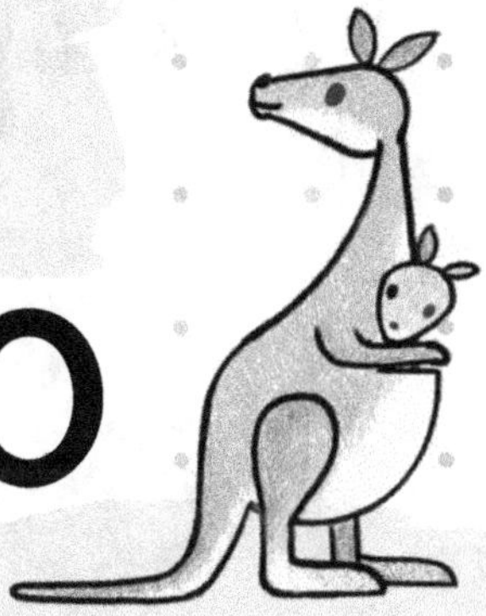

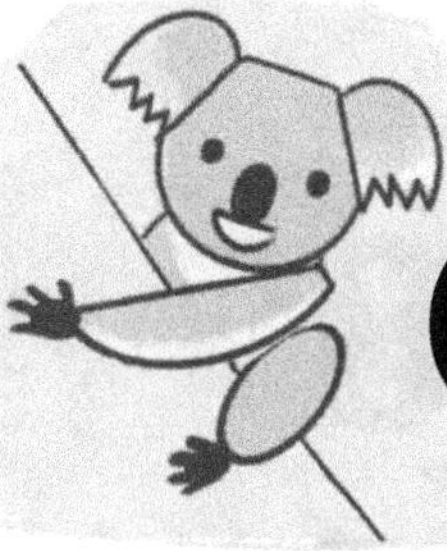

50

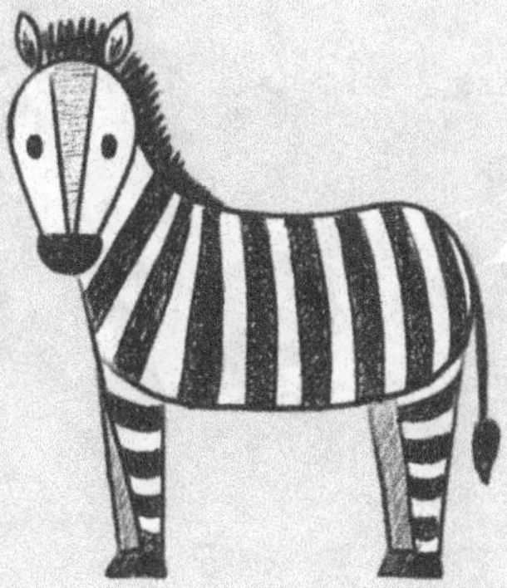

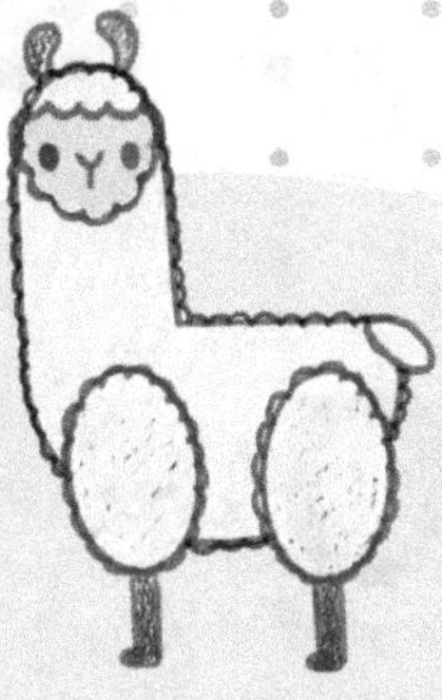

62

52

64

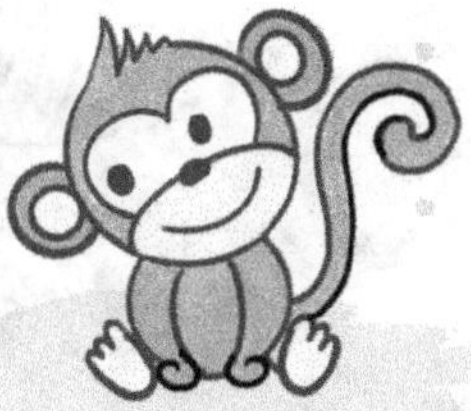

54

66

56

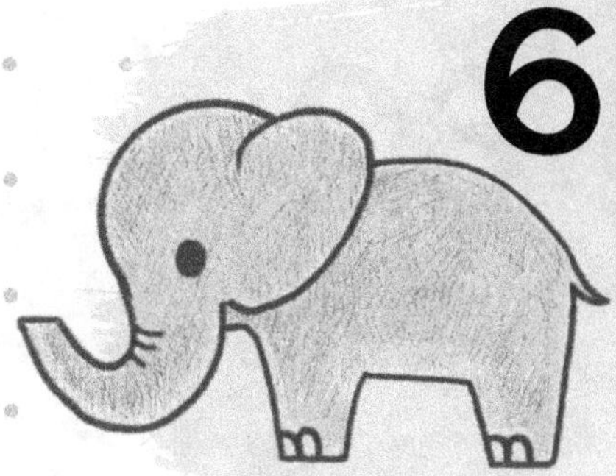

68

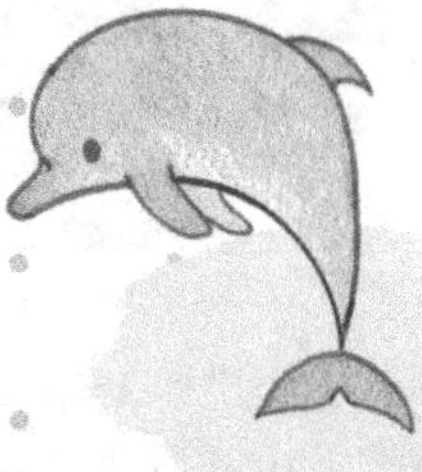

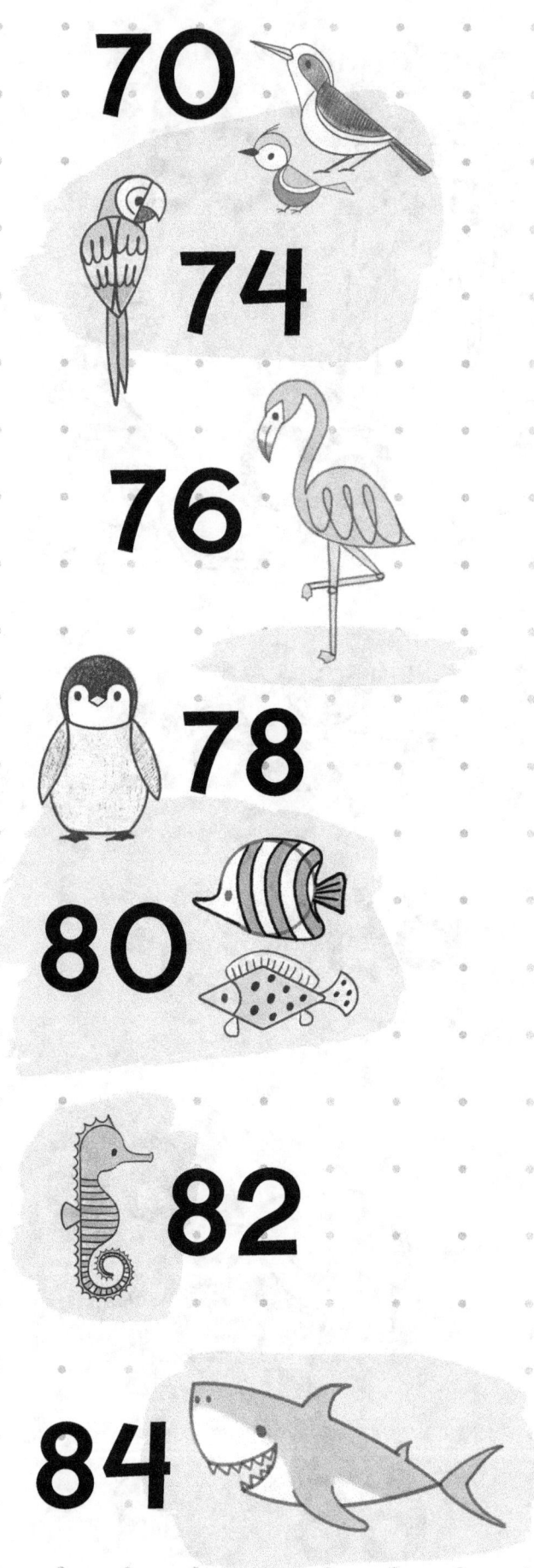

70

74

76

78

80

82

84

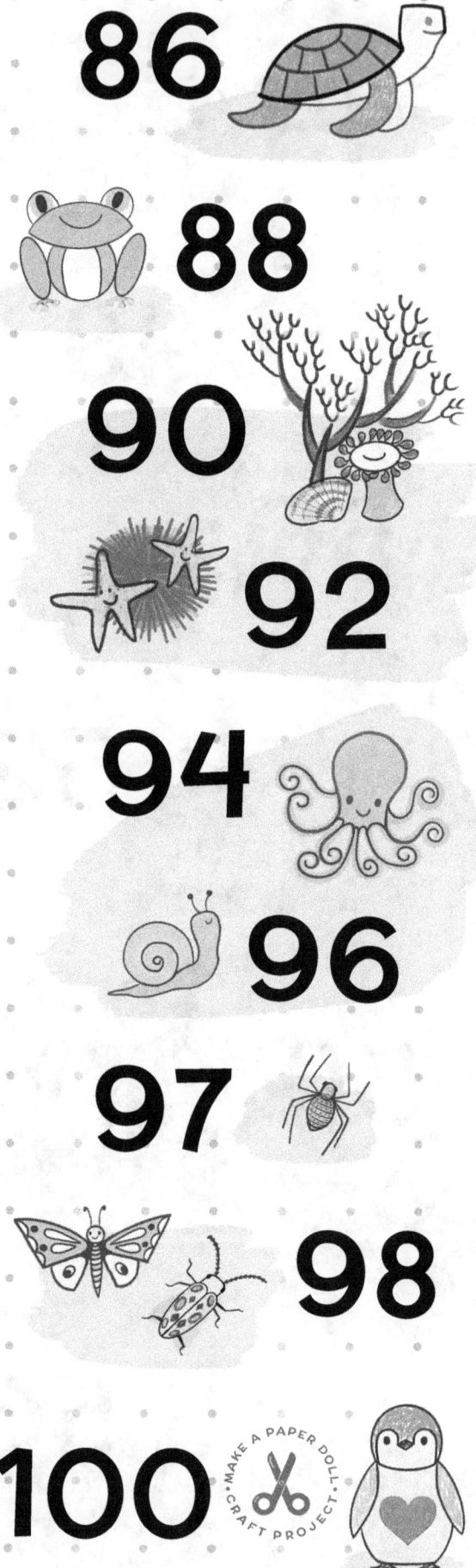

86

88

90

92

94

96

97

98

100

Animals by Alisa Bloom | Draw & Learn™ Book Series

DRAW & LEARN

THINGS YOU NEED

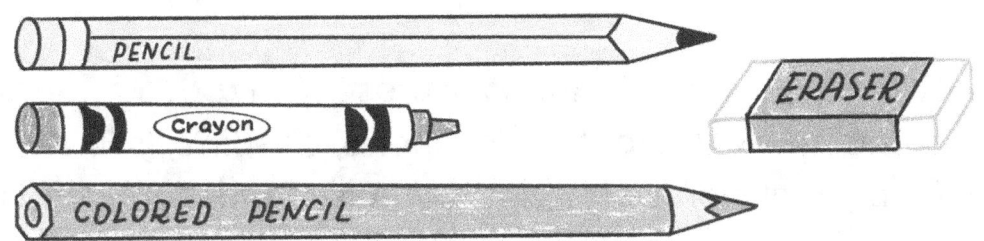

PENCIL

Crayon

COLORED PENCIL

ERASER

HOW IT WORKS

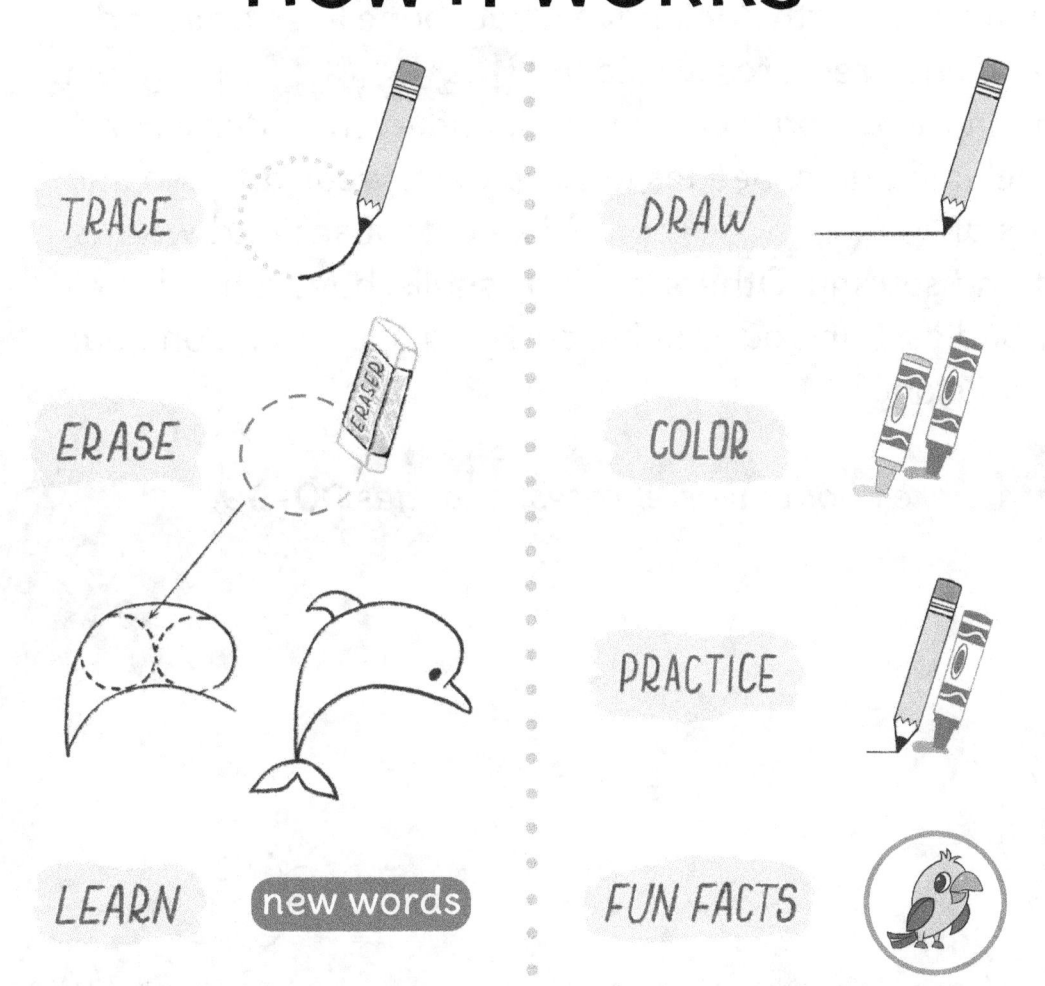

TRACE

ERASE

LEARN new words

DRAW

COLOR

PRACTICE

FUN FACTS

All Kinds of Animals

Animals are living things—they need food, water, and shelter to thrive. Places where animals live and grow are called habitats. Some make their homes on land: deserts, forests, grasslands, and even the tallest mountains. Others live in lakes, rivers, seas, and deep oceans. You can find animals almost everywhere on our beautiful planet.

There are two main groups of animals: those with a backbone inside their bodies and those without. A backbone, or spine, is like a strong bridge made of small bones. It helps animals stand, bend, and move.

Animals without Backbones

Most animals on Earth don't have a backbone like humans do. These amazing creatures are called invertebrates. They can be found in the air, on land, in water, and even underground. Many, including ants, beetles, and spiders, wear a tough suit known as an exoskeleton. Some, like octopuses and worms, are soft and squishy. Others, such as snails, have a hard shell on their bodies. Can you imagine carrying your home on your back all day long?

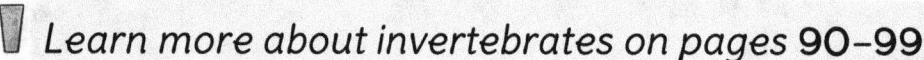

! *Learn more about invertebrates on pages* **90–99.**

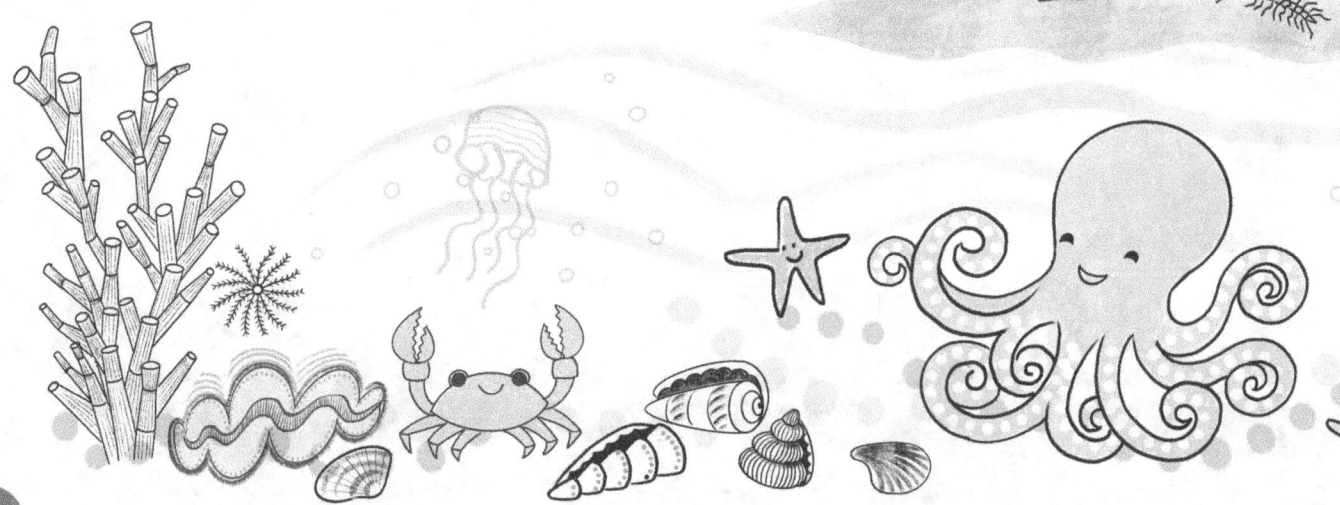

Animals by Alisa Bloom | Draw & Learn™ Book Series

Animals with Backbones

Do you know what mammals, birds, fish, reptiles, and amphibians have in common? They all have a backbone and are called vertebrates. Let's explore what makes these animals and their habitats special.

Mammals

Mammals come in many shapes and sizes, but they all feed their young milk and have hair or fur. They can be as tiny as a mouse or as huge as an elephant. While most mammals are found on land, some, like dolphins and whales, live in water. Did you know you're a mammal, too?

Birds

Birds are the only animals with feathers. They lay their eggs in cozy nests tucked away in trees, bushes, cliffs, or on the ground —any safe place they can find. All birds have wings, but some, like penguins, are unable to fly.

Fish

Fish swim in water and breathe using special organs known as gills. Most fish lay soft, jelly-like eggs, but a few, like sharks, give birth to live babies. Guess what? Many sleep with their eyes open because they have no eyelids!

Reptiles

Reptiles are cold-blooded—they need to soak up the sun to stay warm. Their scaly skin is like armor that keeps them safe. Most have four legs, while some, like snakes, have none. Can you believe reptiles smell with their tongues?

Turn the page to start drawing.

Amphibians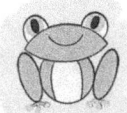

Amphibians, like frogs, toads, and newts, hatch from eggs in water and later move onto land. They don't have hair, fur, or feathers. Instead, they have special skin that helps them breathe and stay wet. Some, like salamanders, can change colors and grow back lost tails.

Lines and Shapes

Copy these lines.

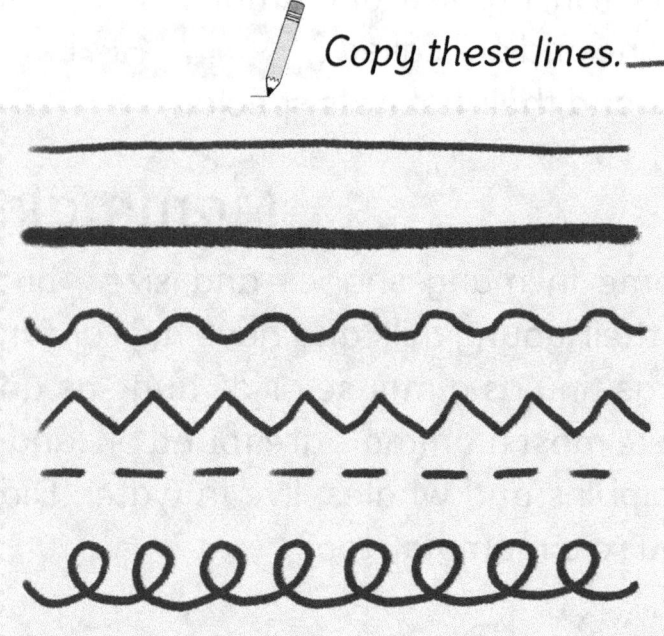

Shapes are made of lines. Practice drawing these shapes.

Trace this.

Now you try.

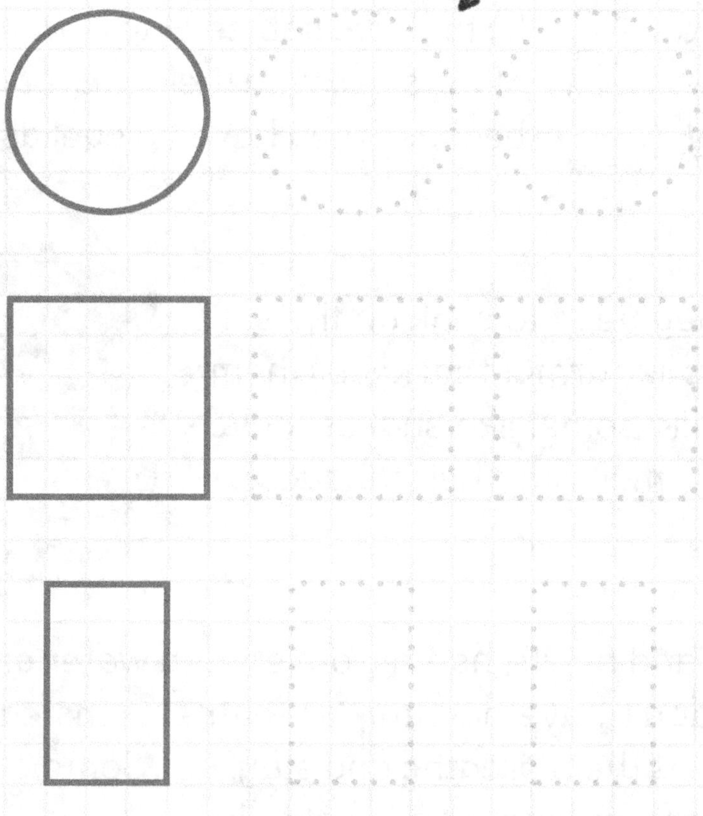

Shapes are all around us. Everything you see is made of shapes like circles, rectangles, squares, and triangles. Artists use shapes to draw animals, plants, rocks, buildings, and even cool machines like rockets.

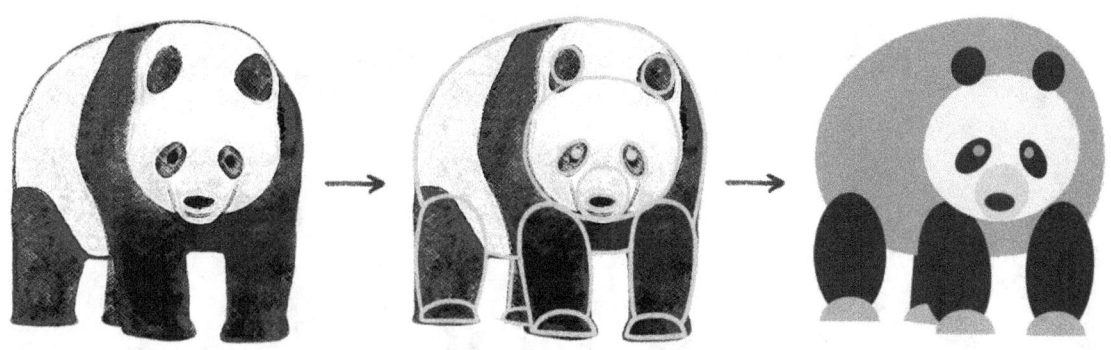

! Can you find the shapes used in this giant panda drawing?

Trace this. ↘

Now you try. ↘

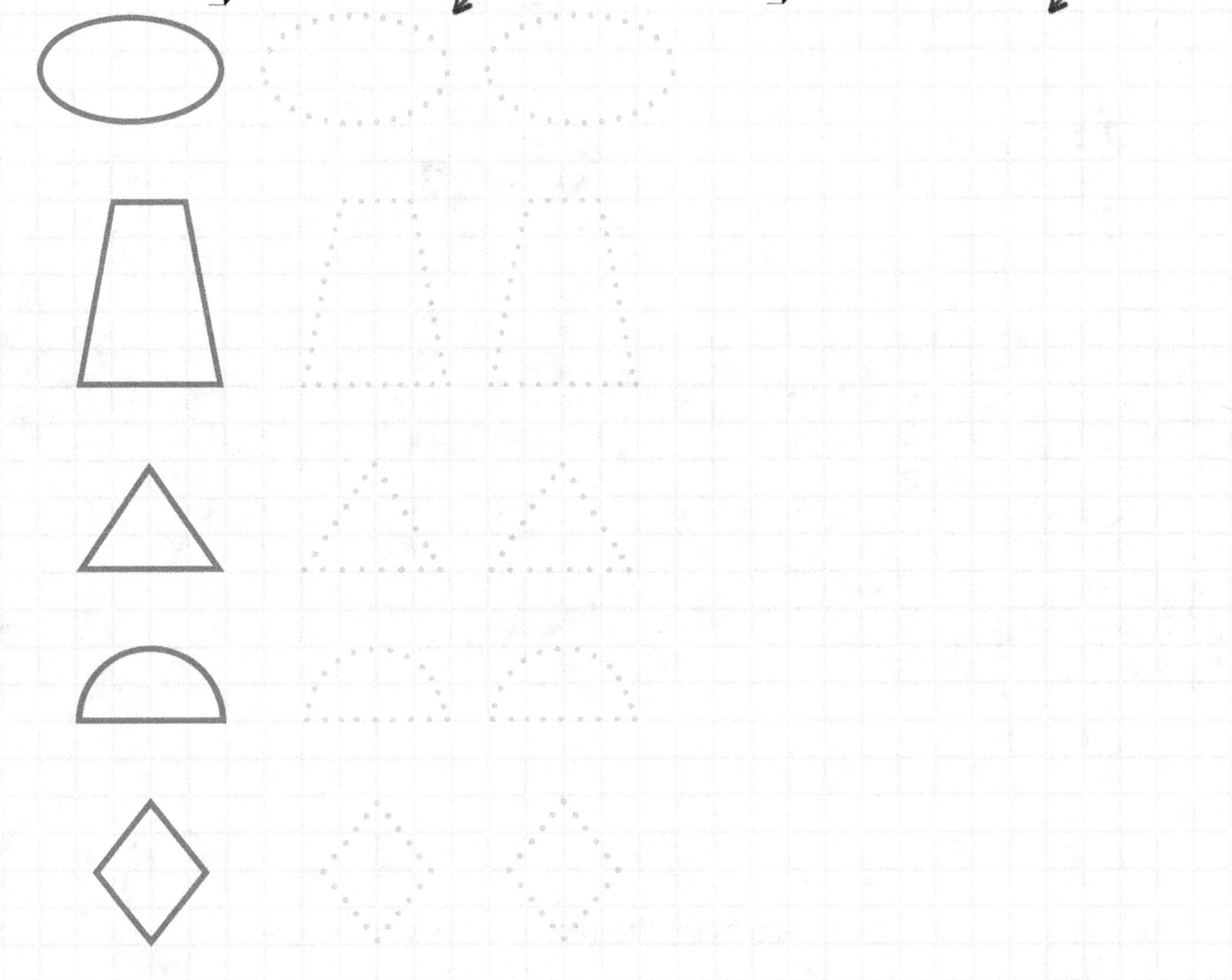

Lines can be THIN or **THICK**.

 Use thin and thick lines to copy these drawings.

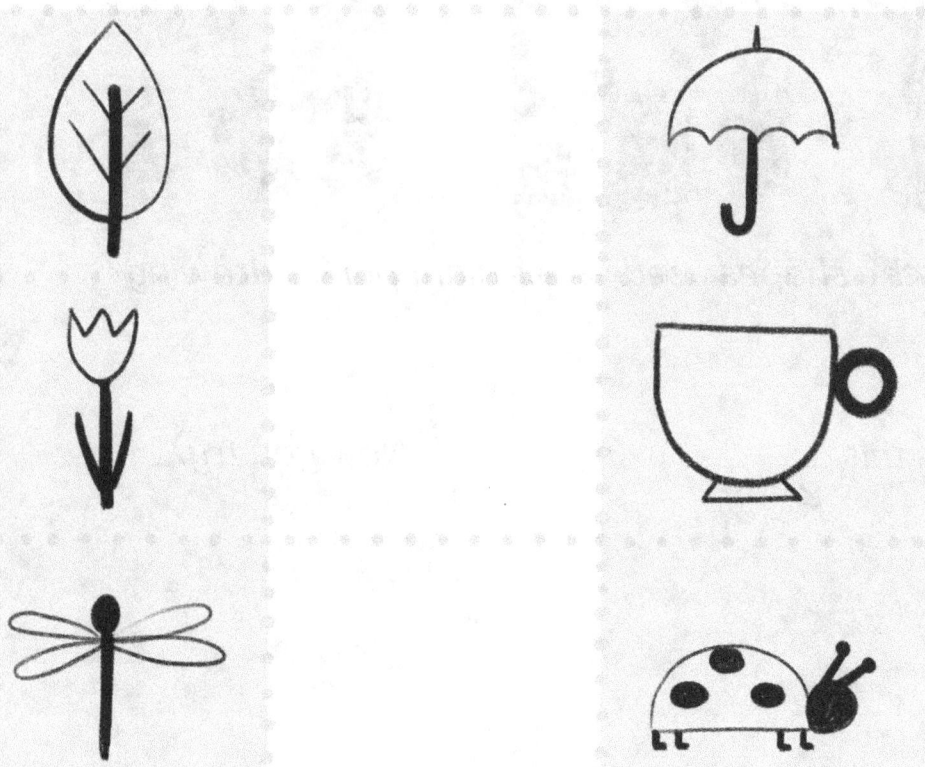

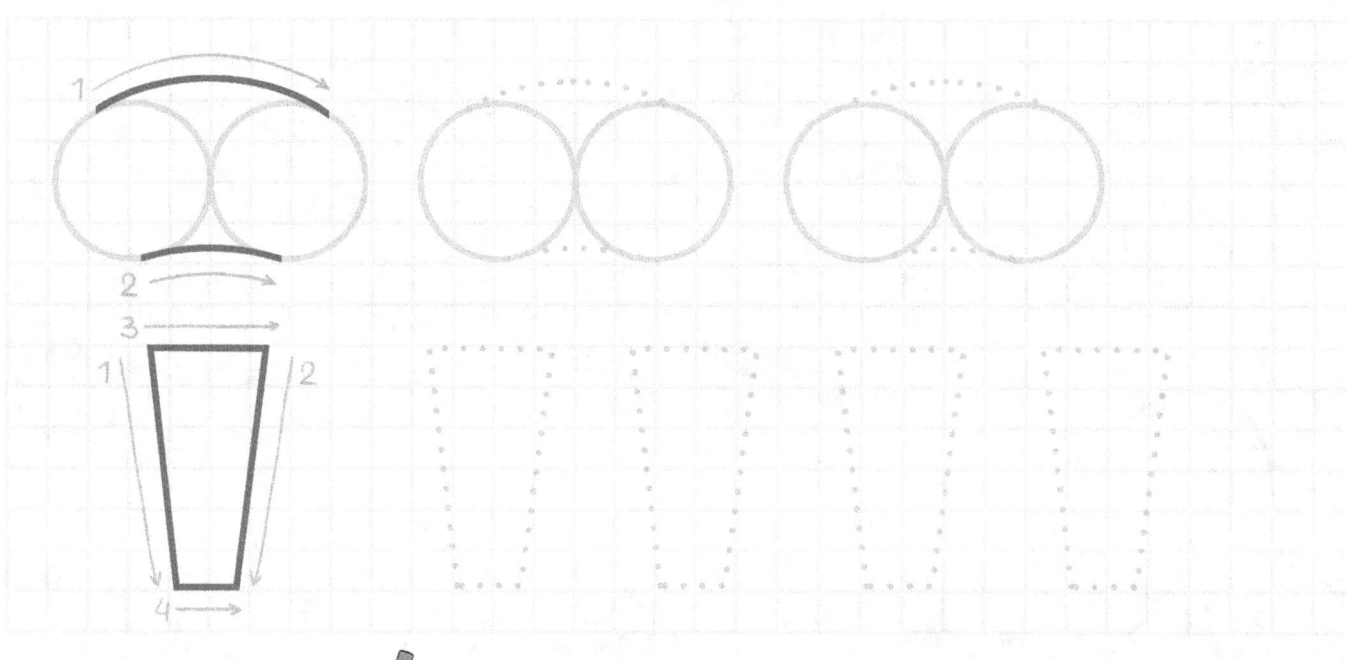

 Trace over the dotted lines.

Animals by Alisa Bloom | Draw & Learn™ Book Series

Shapes can be **BIG** or SMALL.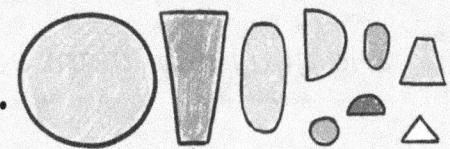

Trace this.

Now you try.

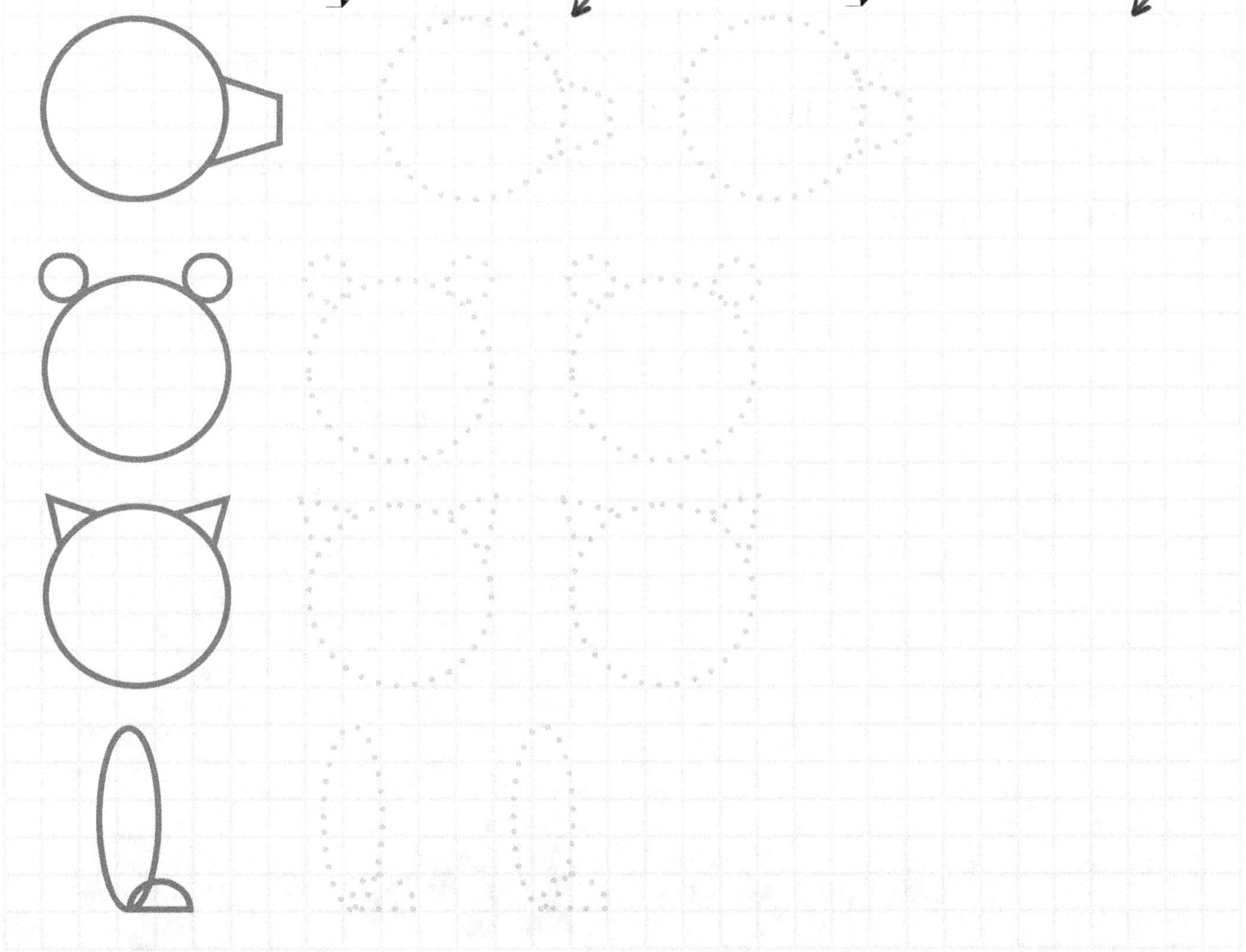

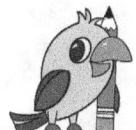 *Next, let's practice drawing some amazing animals.*

Begin each lesson by tracing the dotted shapes with a pencil. Then, copy the black lines and erase the dashed parts as shown in each step. The gray lines show what's already been drawn. Finally, color your drawing with colored pencils or crayons. Let's draw, learn, and have fun!

 You can use graph paper to make extra copies of the drawings.

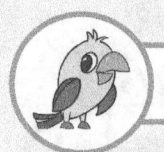 *Did you know giant pandas spend half a day eating?*

Panda bears, also called giant pandas, live in bamboo forests high up in the mountains. They're part of the bear family, just like black bears, brown bears, and polar bears. Pandas have big white heads, black ears, and black patches around their eyes. These gentle bears don't move around much—they spend most of their time napping or munching on bamboo. Even though they're big, pandas are great climbers and can swim surprisingly well.

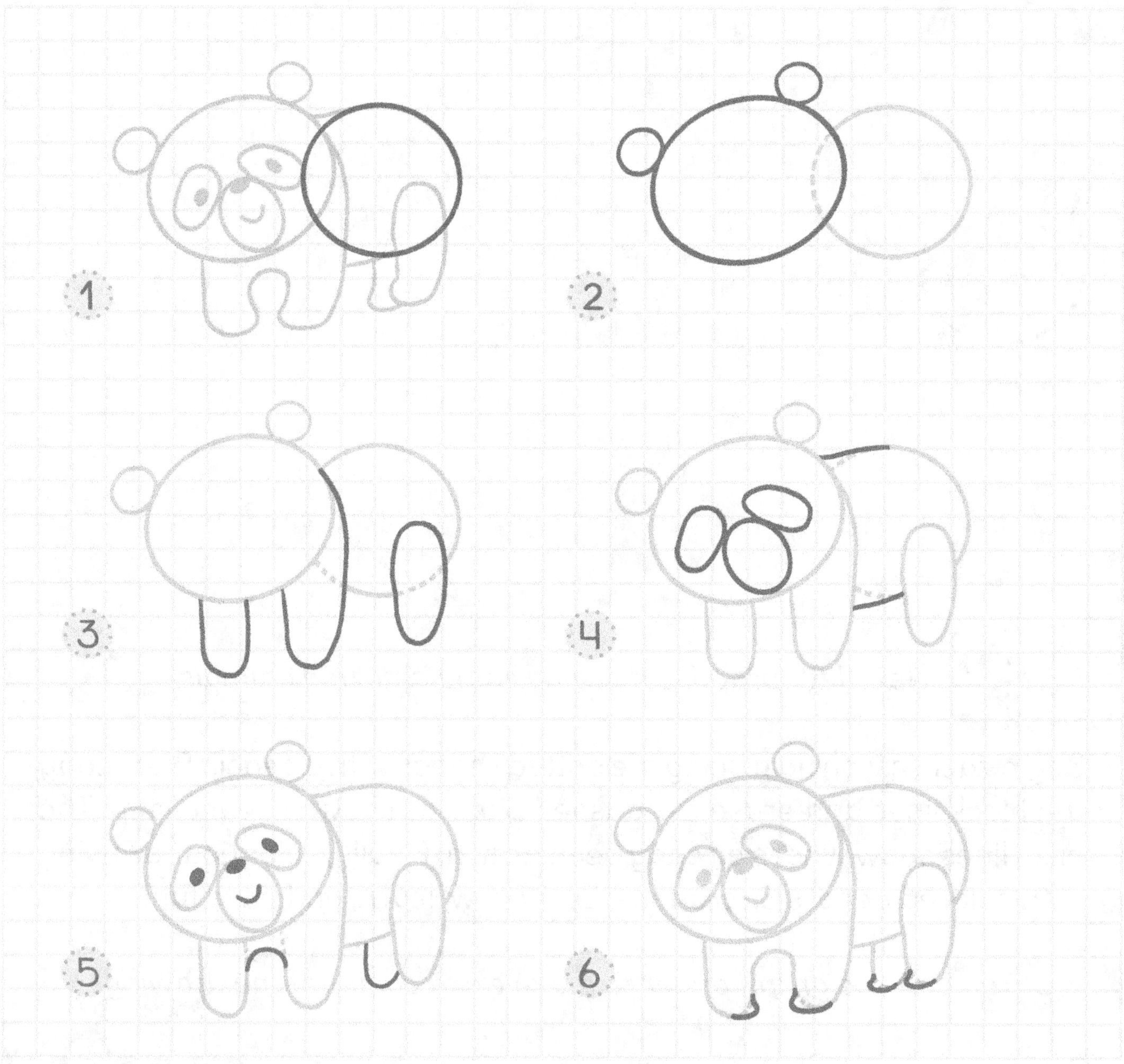

1

2

3

4

5

6

Animals by Alisa Bloom | Draw & Learn™ Book Series

PANDA

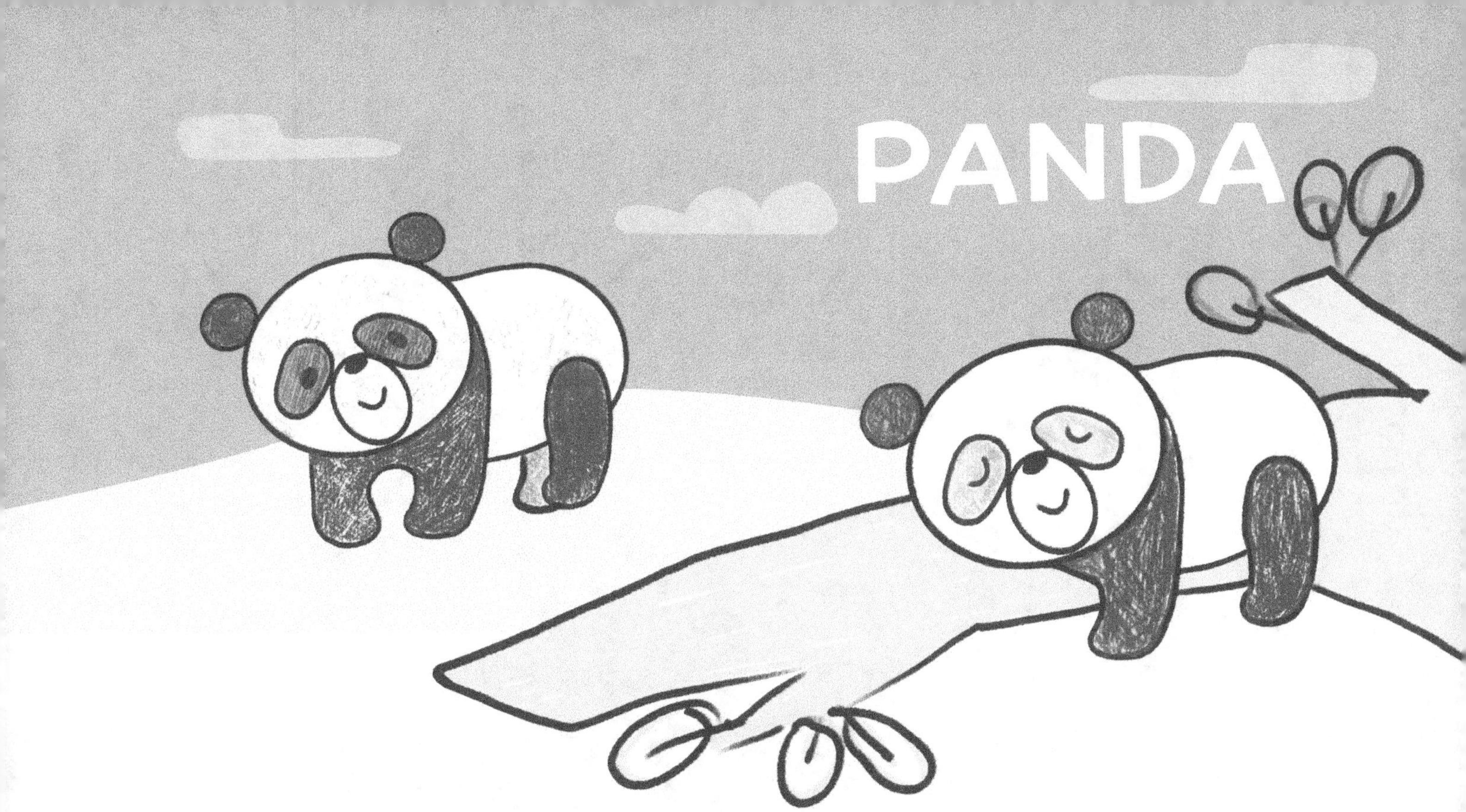

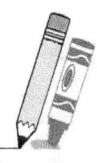

Your turn to draw a giant panda. Trace the shape above to get started.

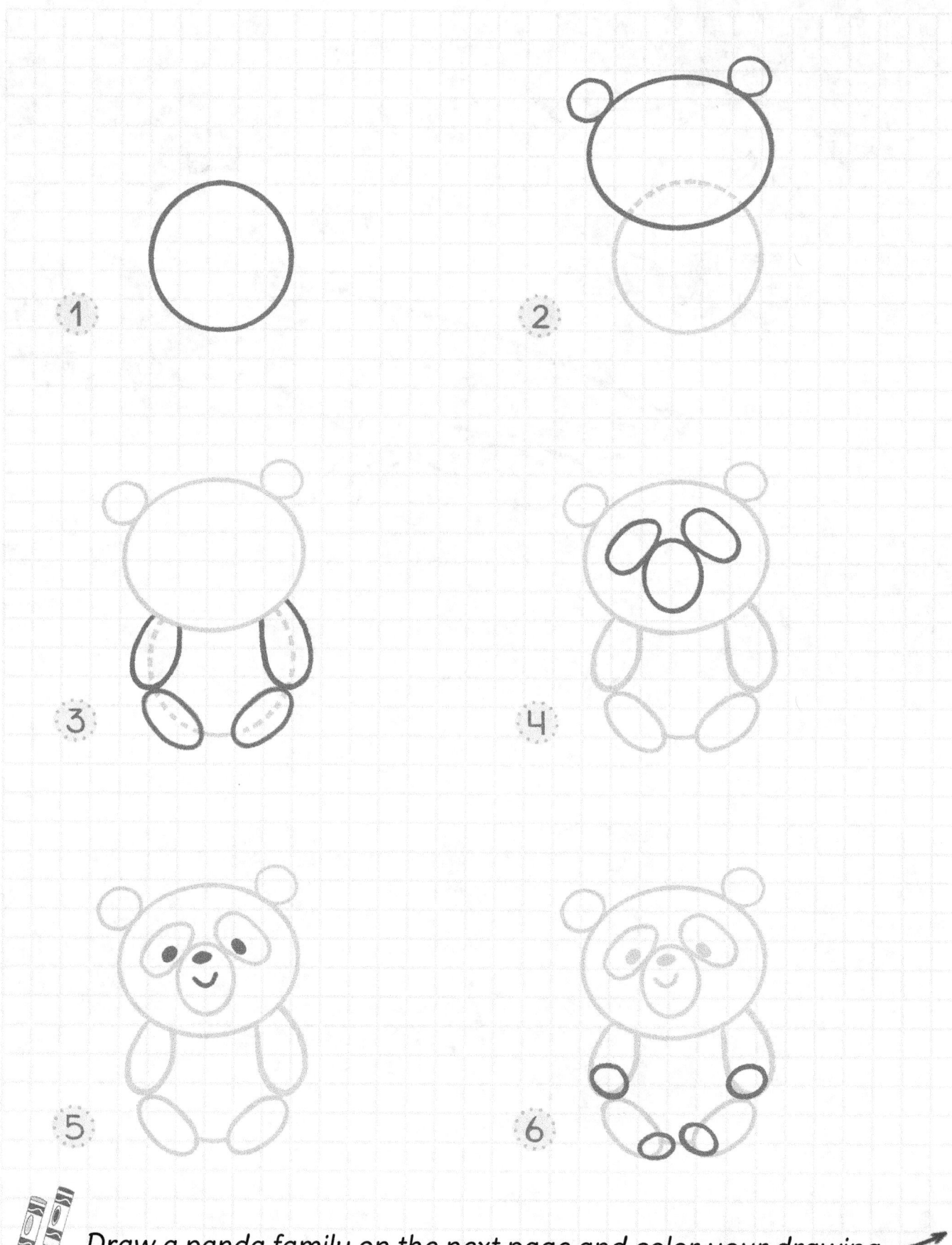

1

2

3

4

5

6

Draw a panda family on the next page and color your drawing.

Animals by Alisa Bloom | Draw & Learn™ Book Series

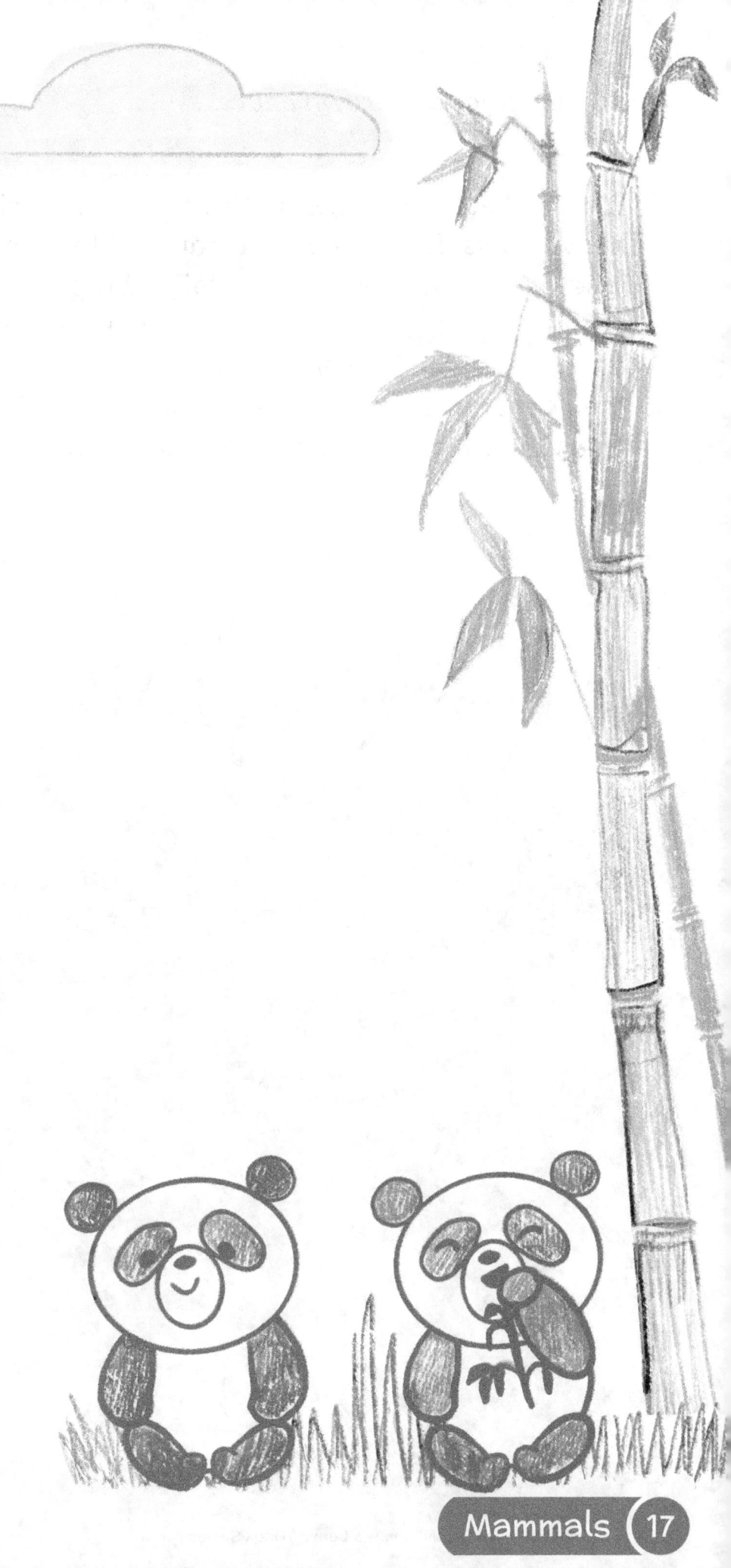

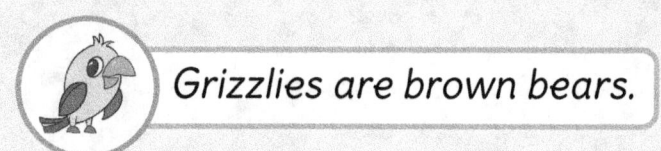

Grizzlies are brown bears.

Brown bears are some of the largest land animals, with big heads and heavy paws. In summer, you can find them in forests and near rivers, where they look for food. In fall, they prepare for a long winter nap called hibernation . They snuggle up in cozy dens all winter and wake up in spring feeling very hungry. These furry giants are omnivores — they eat both plants and meat. They especially love honey and salmon. Their keen sense of smell helps them sniff out food from far away.

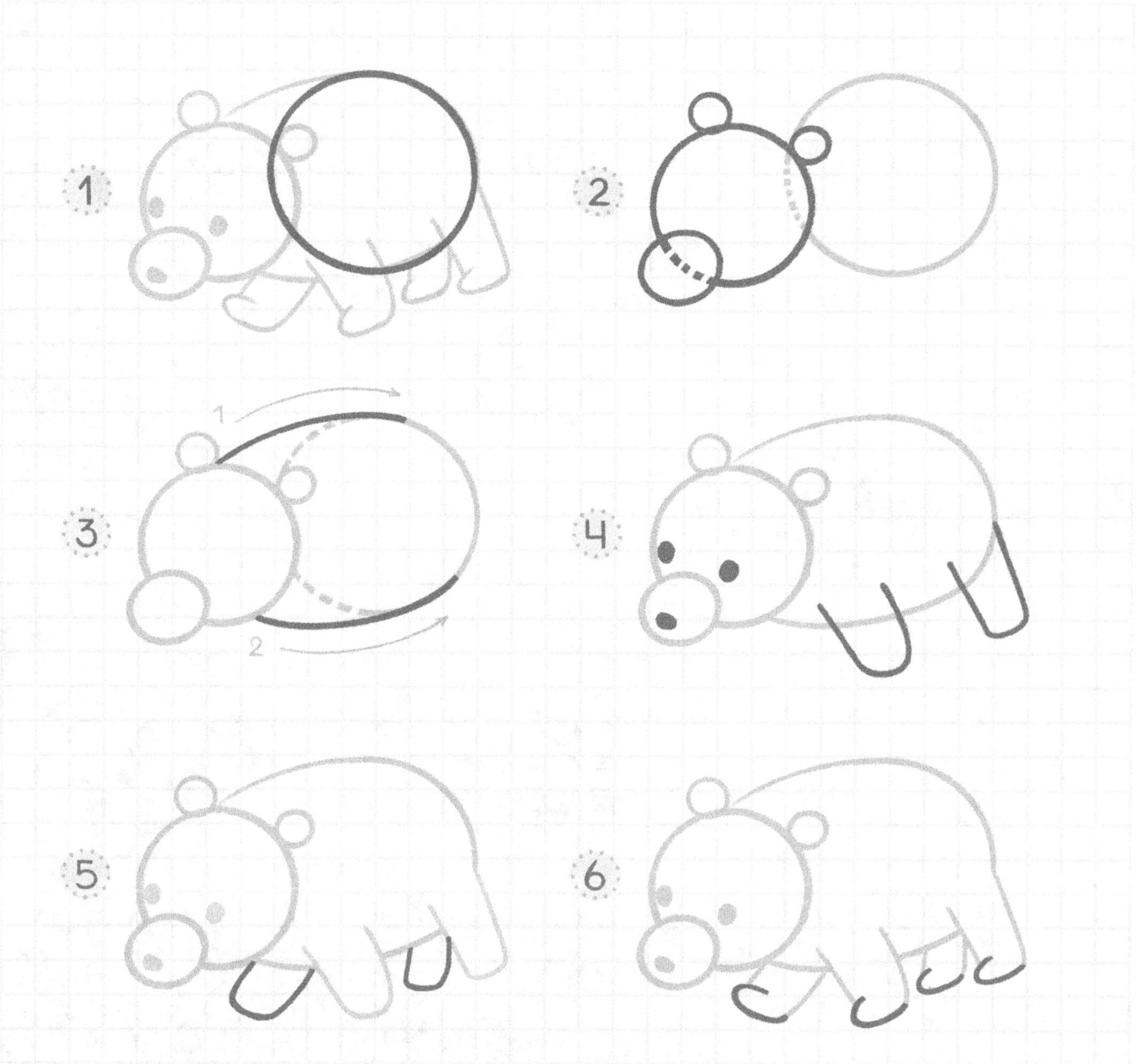

BEAR

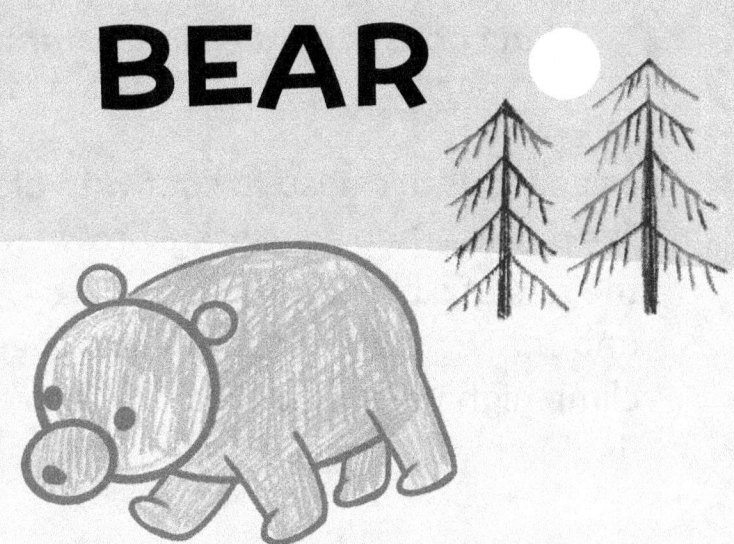

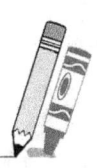 *Your turn to draw a brown bear.*

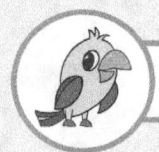 *Raccoons are excellent swimmers.*

Raccoons are easy to spot with black patches on their faces that look like masks. They have gray-brown fur, bushy striped tails, and are about the size of a big cat. Raccoons are (nocturnal)—they nap during the day and stay active at night. These clever animals use their paws to dig dens, climb high walls, and squeeze through small spaces. They're experts at finding food—they can open doors, jars, and even trash cans.

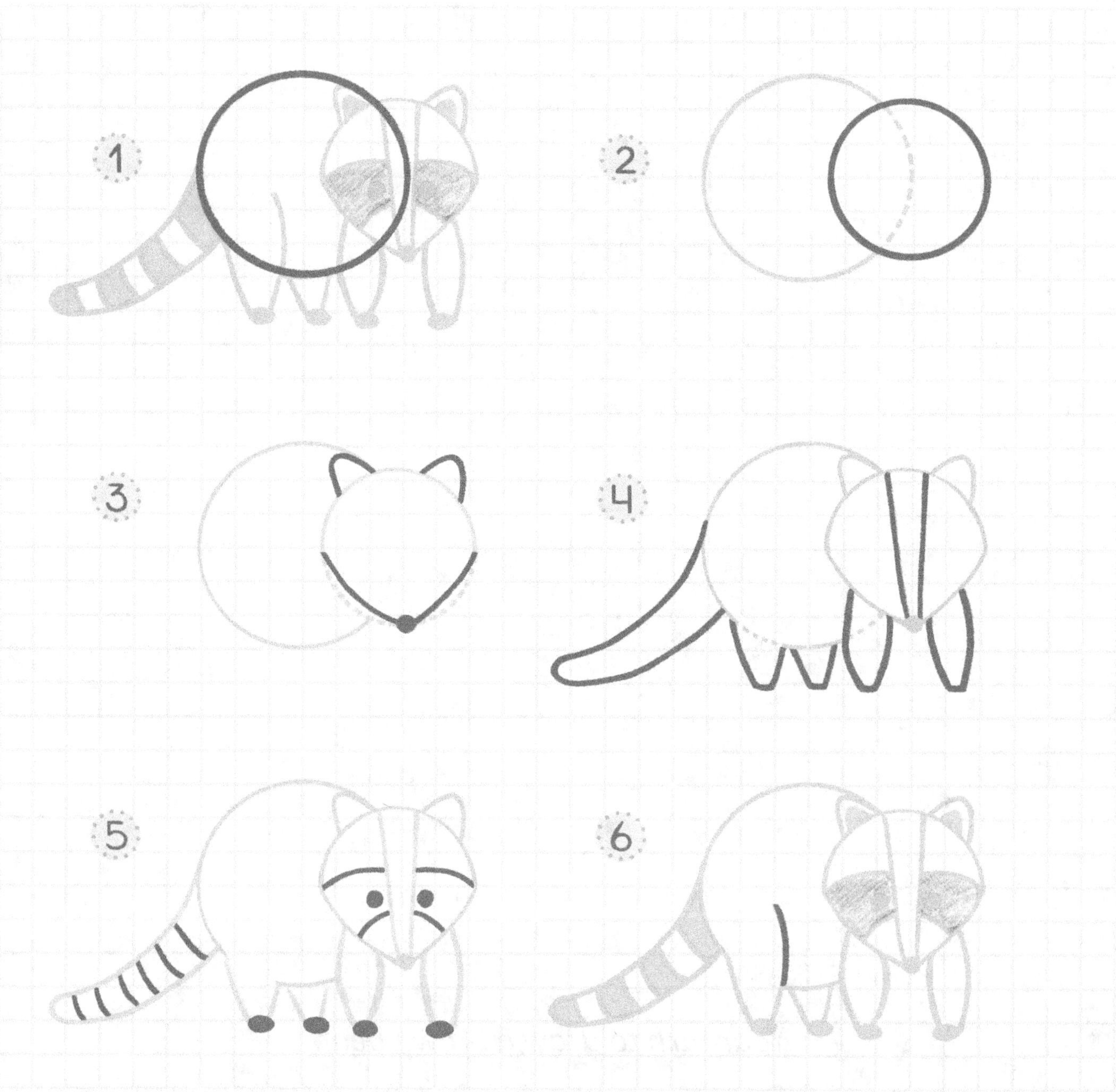

1

2

3

4

5

6

Animals by Alisa Bloom | Draw & Learn™ Book Series

RACCOON

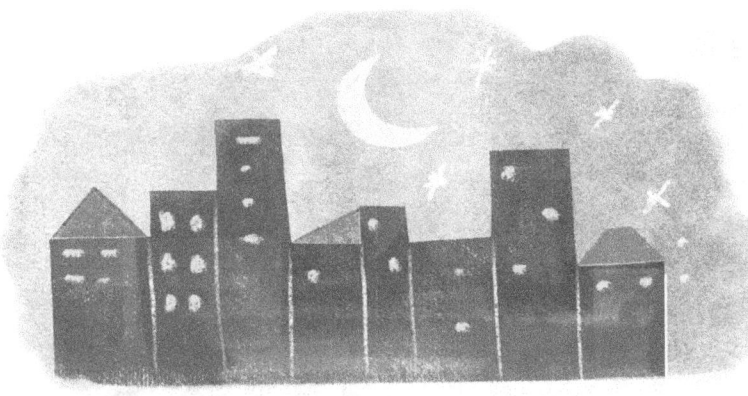

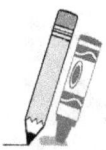 *Draw a raccoon in a city.*

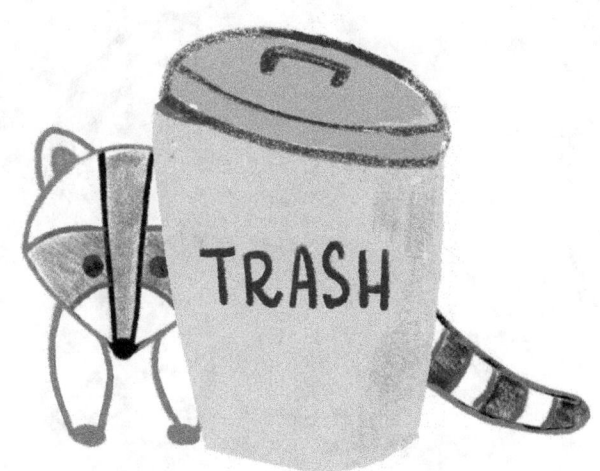

TRASH

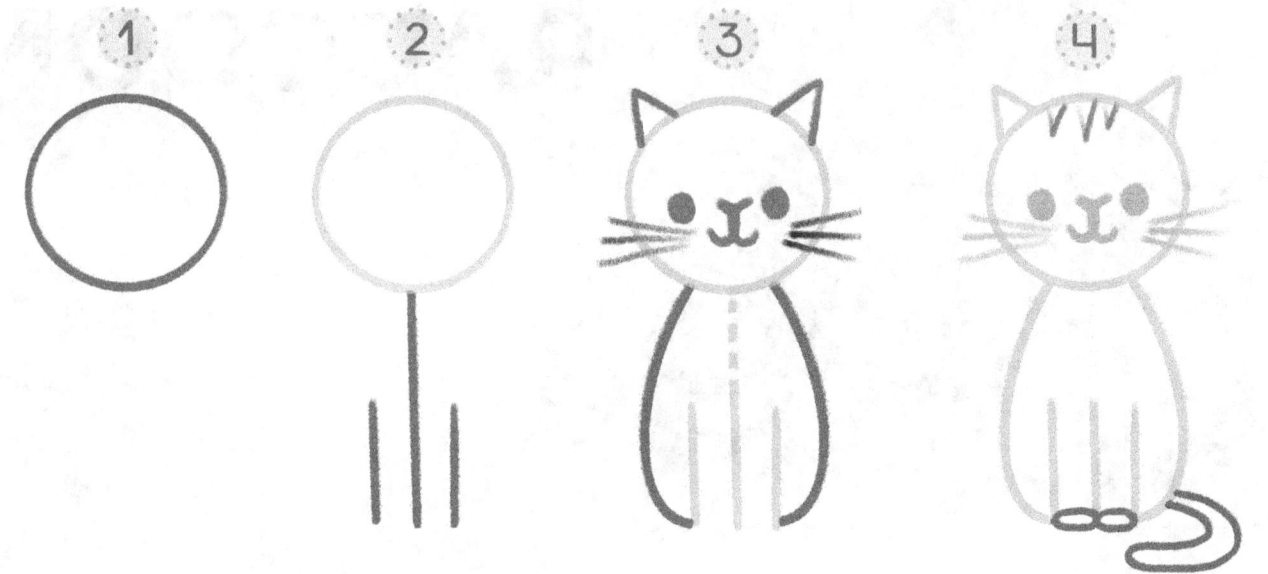

1

2

3

4

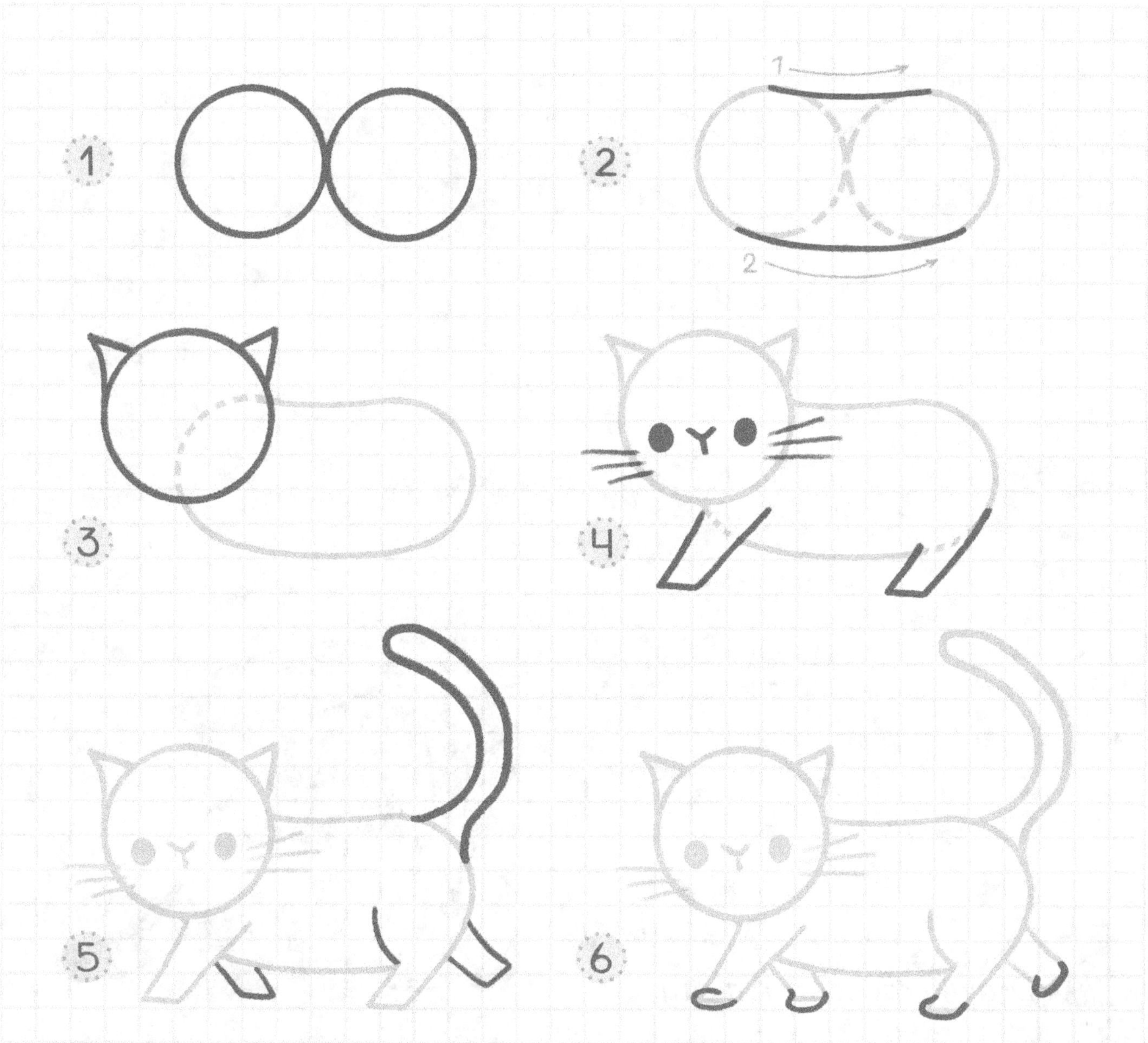

5

6

Animals by Alisa Bloom | Draw & Learn™ Book Series

CAT

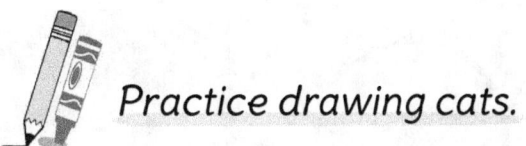

Practice drawing cats.

Cats are curious furry friends that love playing and exploring, but they also enjoy sleeping and resting. **Kittens**, or baby cats, are so adorable—they look like fluffy balls with blue eyes! Cats use their strong legs to jump and climb with ease. With their excellent balance, they can land safely on their feet from high places. Their whiskers are like special antennae that guide them in the dark and through tight spots.

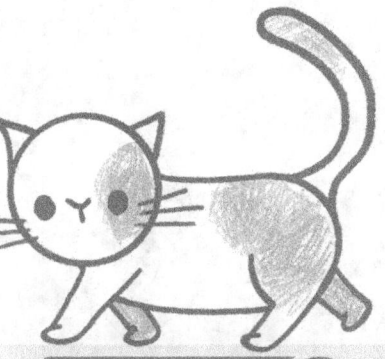

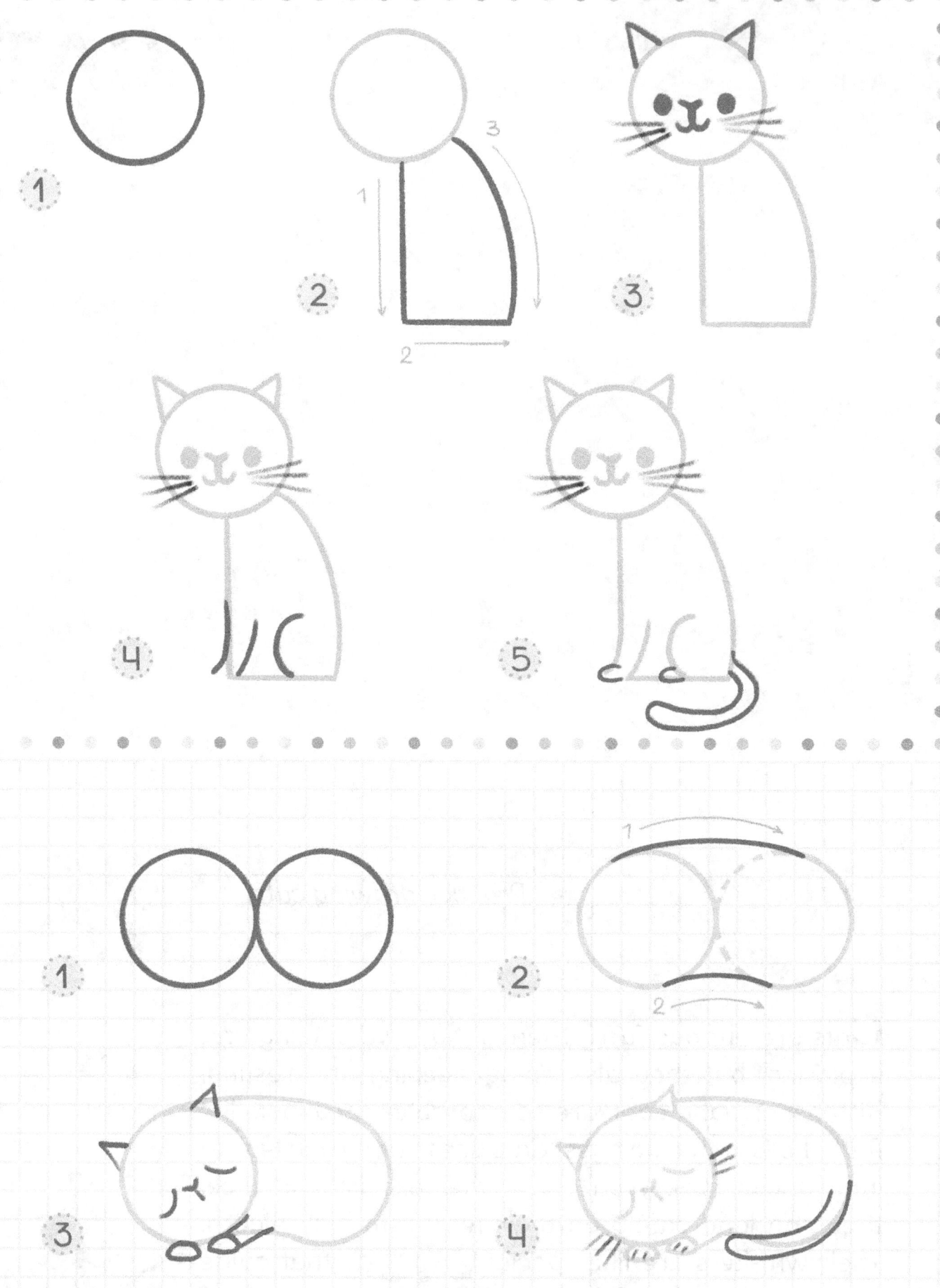

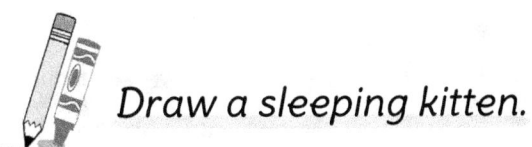 *Draw a sleeping kitten.*

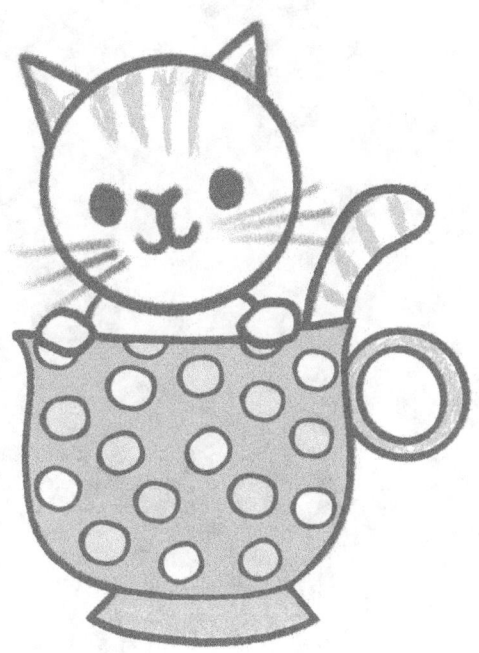

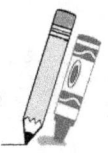 *Draw a cat in a cup.*

Animal Patterns

Patterns are shapes, lines, or colors that repeat. Many animals have spots, stripes, patches, or other special markings on their bodies. These patterns help them stay hidden in their surroundings. This is known as camouflage —it's like playing hide-and-seek while dressed in colors that make you hard to spot. An animal that hunts others for food is called a predator , while those hunted by the predator are called prey . Both predators and prey use camouflage to stay out of sight.

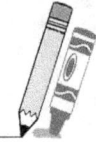 *Find and draw the missing patterns on these animals.*

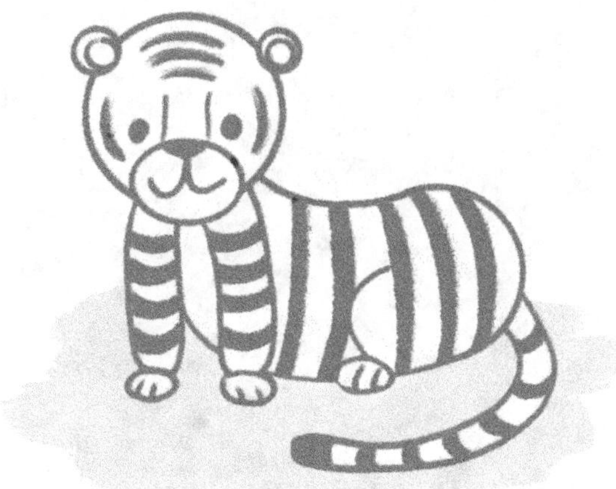

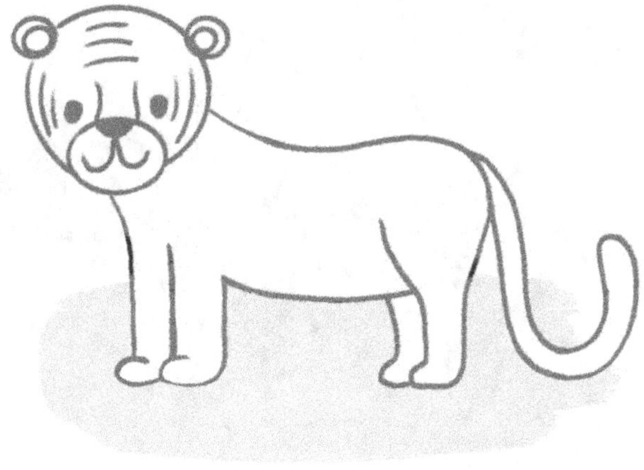

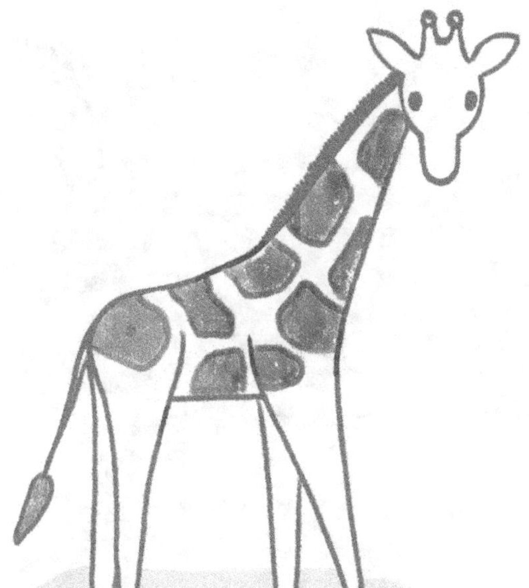

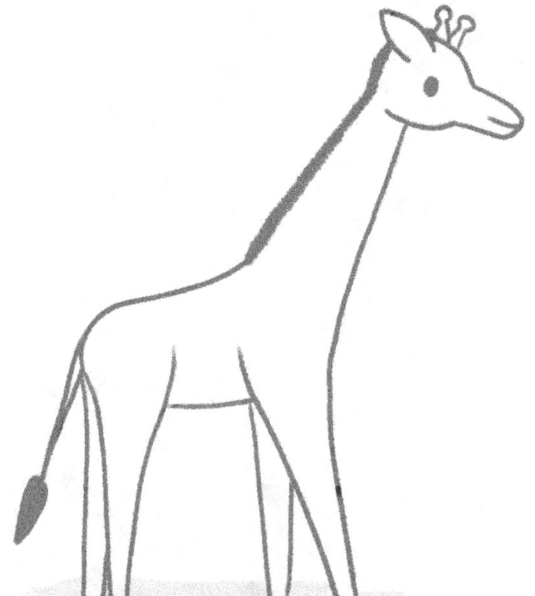

Animals by Alisa Bloom | Draw & Learn™ Book Series

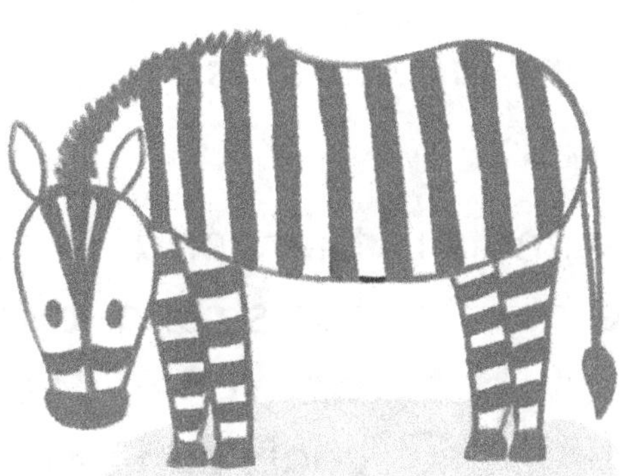

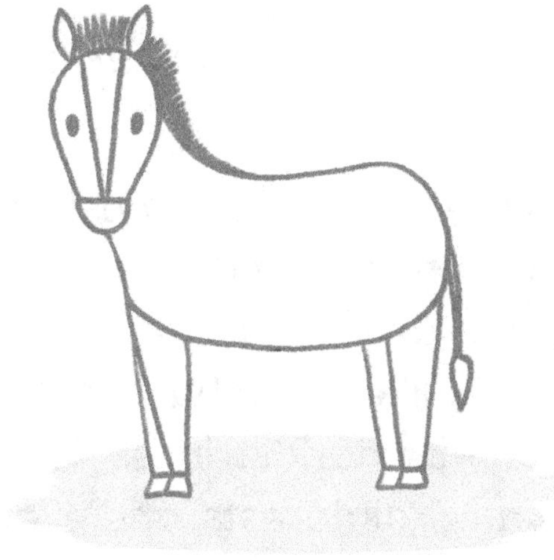

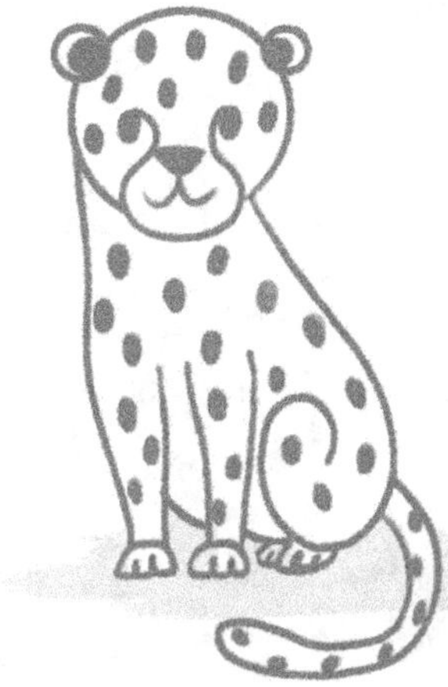

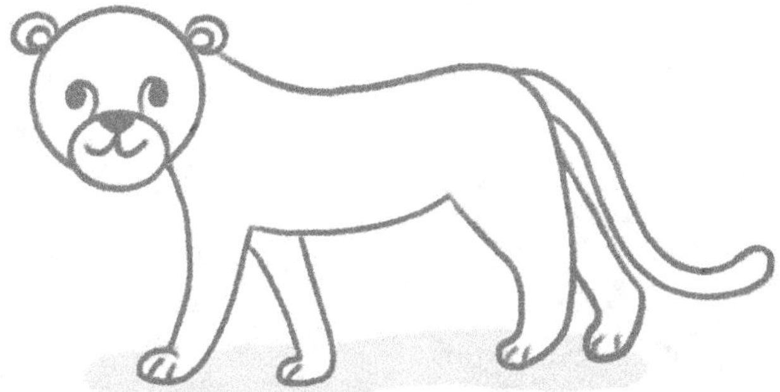

Turn the page to learn how to draw these big cats. →

Big Cats

Cheetahs, jaguars, leopards, lions, and tigers belong to the big cat family. Tigers are the largest, and cheetahs are the smallest. Big cats take great care of their babies, called **cubs**, keeping them safe and well-fed. They're carnivores and eat mostly meat. Big cats are excellent hunters with sharp hearing and a strong sense of smell.

TIGER   LION   CHEETAH

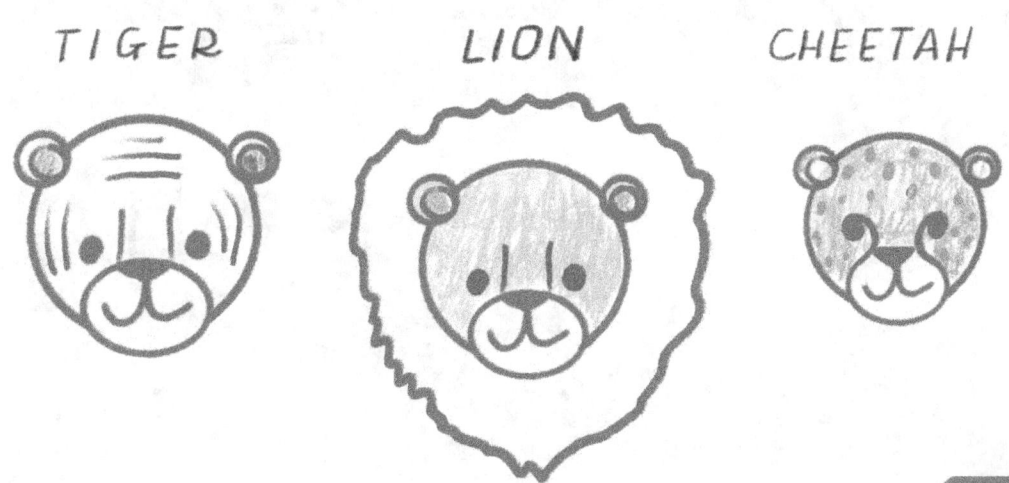

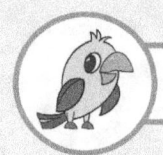

Tigers are some of the most powerful animals in the world. They can leap far, run fast, and swim across wide rivers. With strong jaws, big paws, and razor-sharp claws, they can easily catch antelopes, deer, and larger prey like water buffalo. Their beautiful, thick coats can be orange or white with dark stripes. Tigers are found in many places, including grasslands, rainforests, and even cold, snowy woodlands.

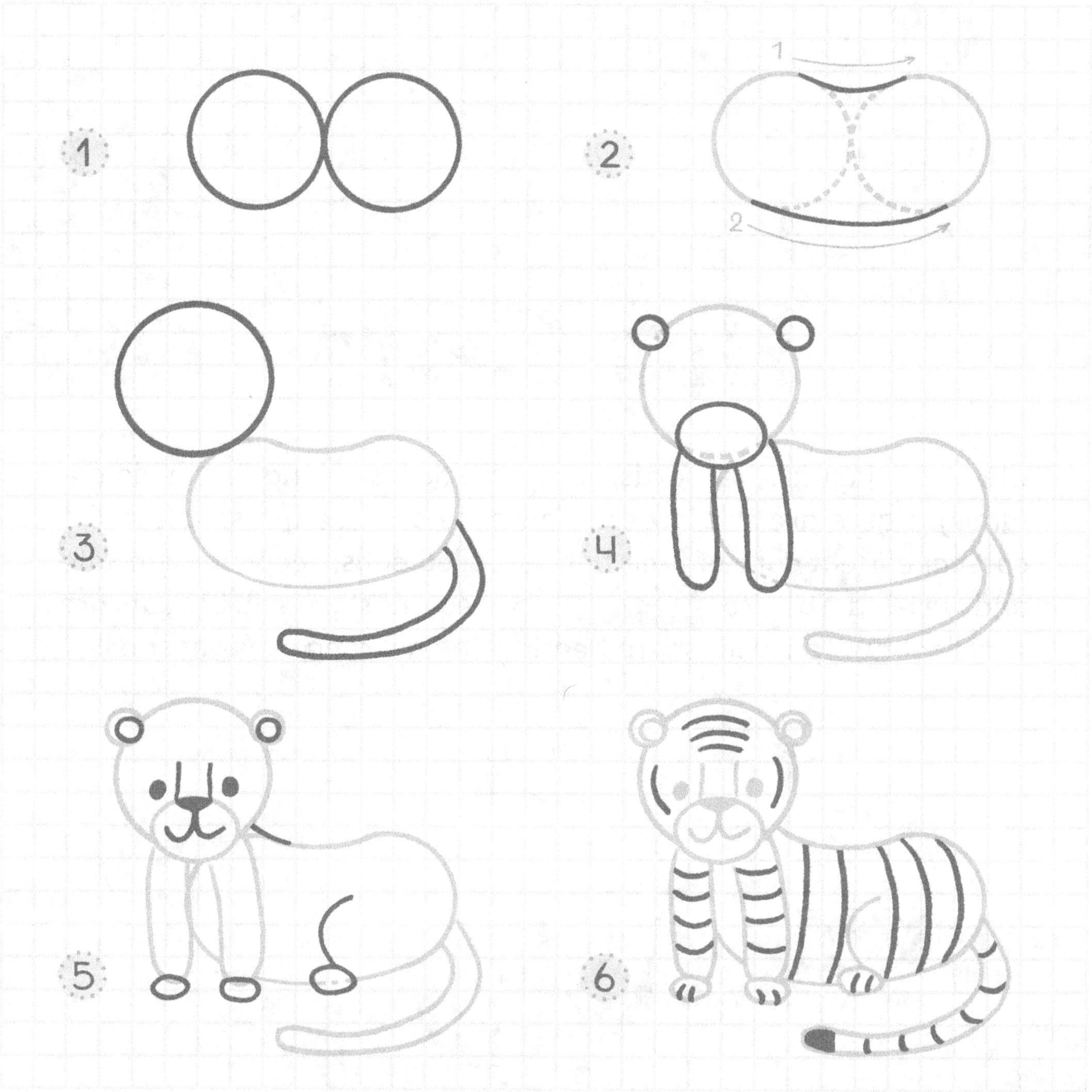

1

2

1
2

3

4

5

6

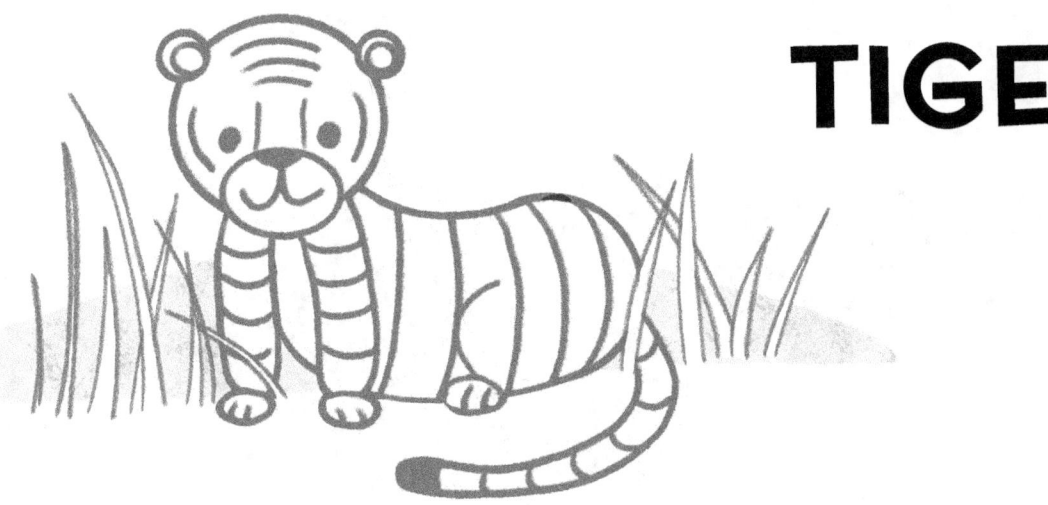

TIGER

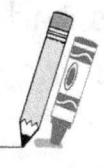 *Draw a tiger sitting on a grassy hill.*

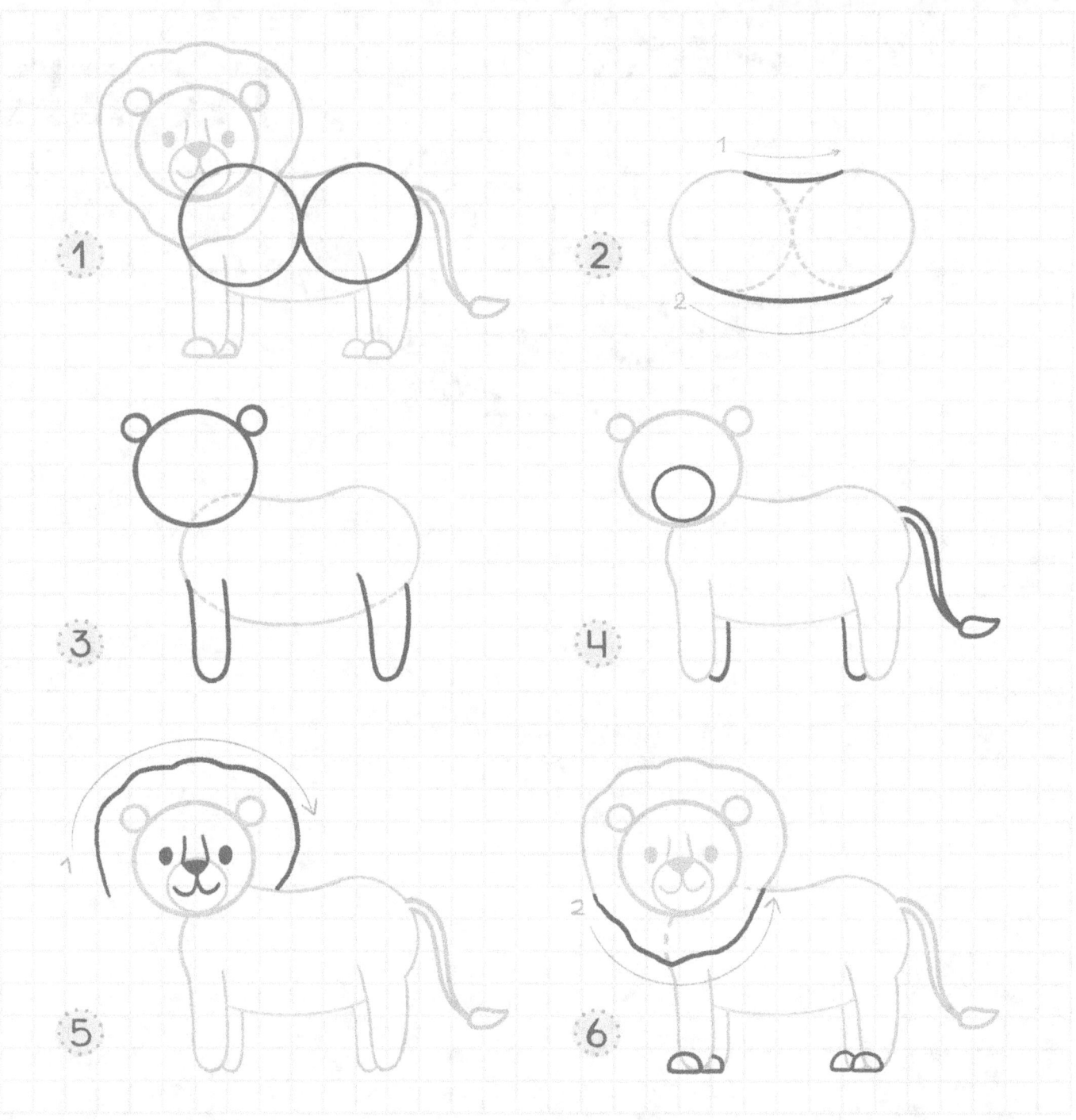

Lions are big cats with loud roars that sound like thunder. They're the second-largest cats, after Siberian tigers. Most lions live in warm, grassy places called savannas. They have yellow-brown fur, short legs, and long tails tipped with black hair. Their big heads sport round golden eyes and a large black nose. Did you know only male lions grow manes? Lion cubs are born with spots that help them hide in bushes and tall grass. As they grow, the spots fade. Cubs learn to hunt by watching their mom and other lions in their family, called a **pride**.

Animals by Alisa Bloom | Draw & Learn™ Book Series

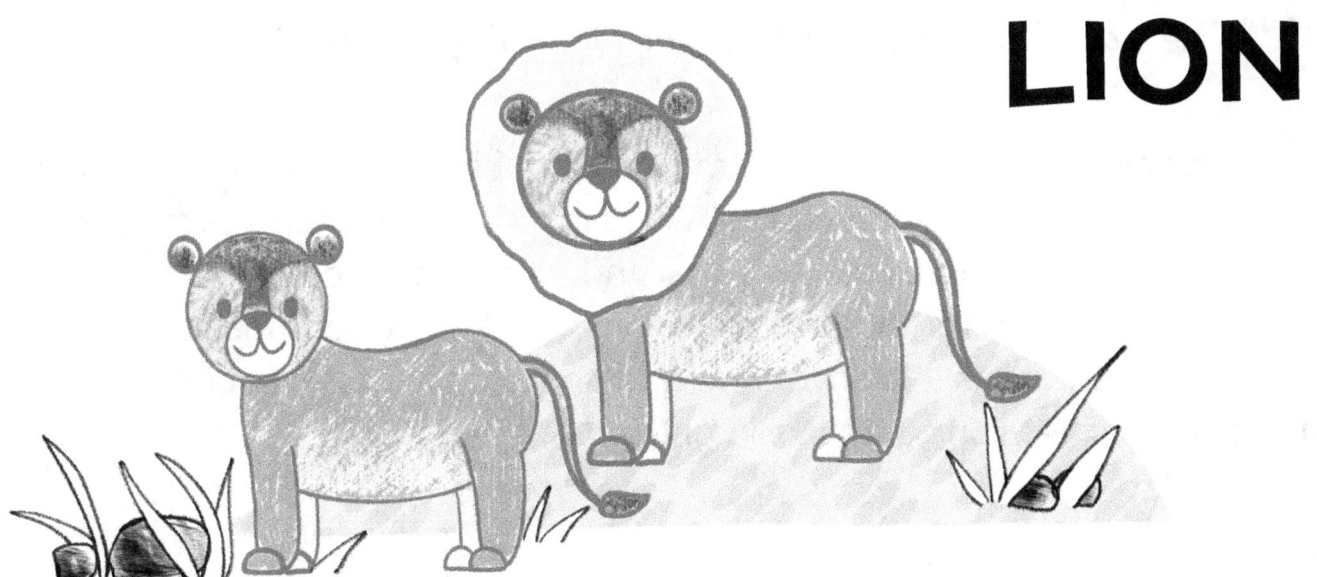

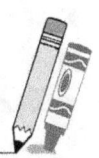 *Your turn to draw a lion and a lioness.*

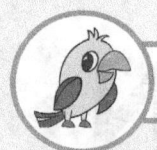 *The black lines on a cheetah's face look like tear marks.*

Cheetahs are the fastest land mammals, able to run as fast as race cars. They use their sharp eyesight and incredible speed to catch prey. These sleek cats have small heads and slim bodies covered in black spots. Each cheetah's spot pattern is one of a kind. Cheetahs are found in large open areas like savannas and some deserts. They're the only big cats, besides lions, that live in groups.

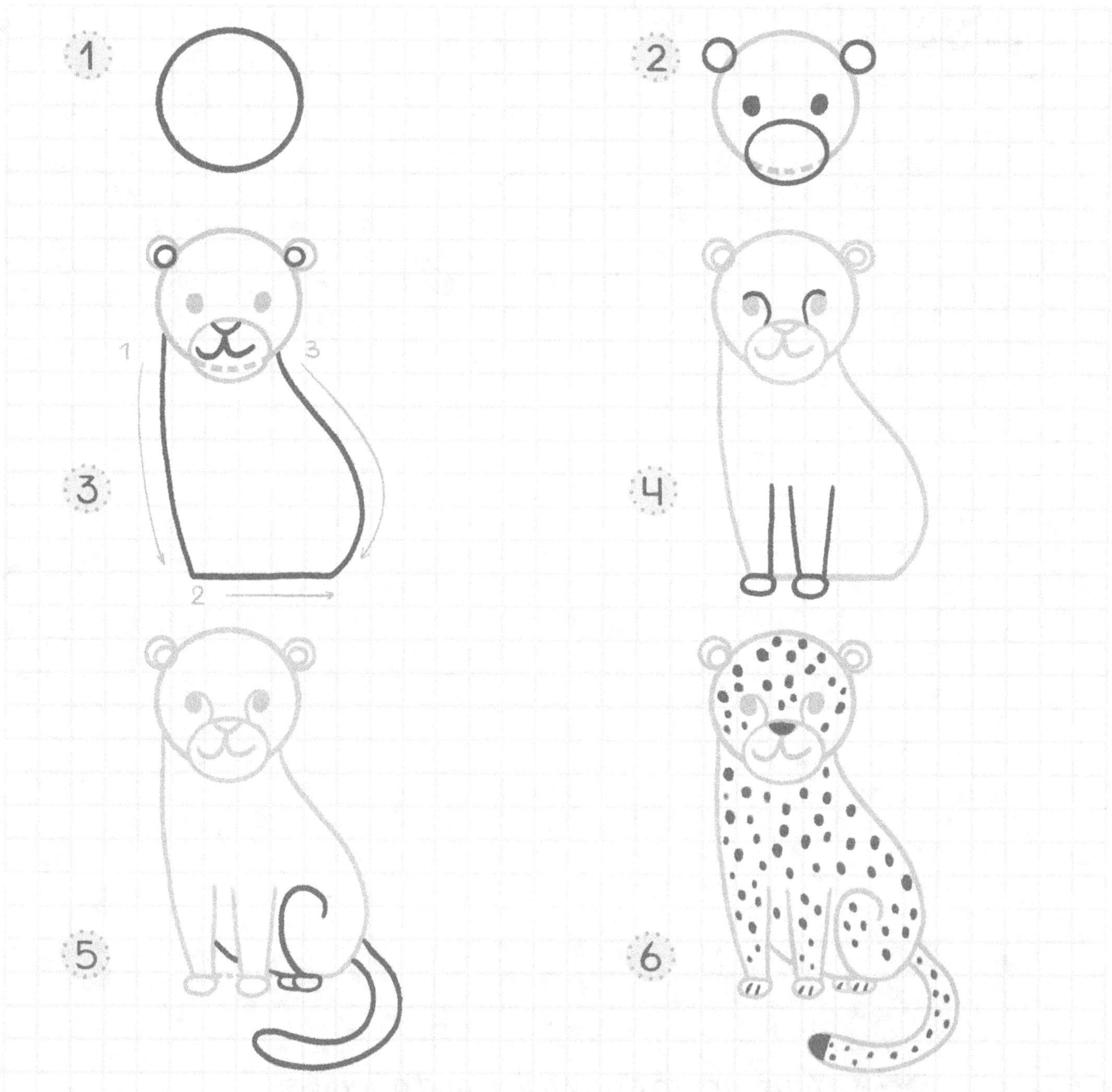

1

2

3

4

5

6

CHEETAH

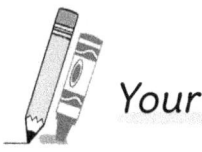 *Your turn to draw cheetahs.*

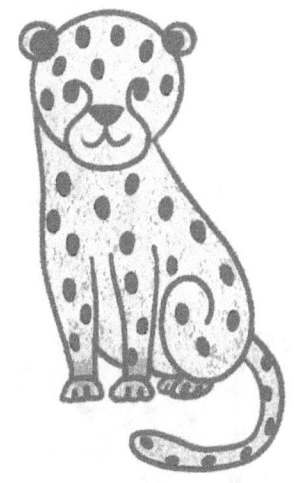

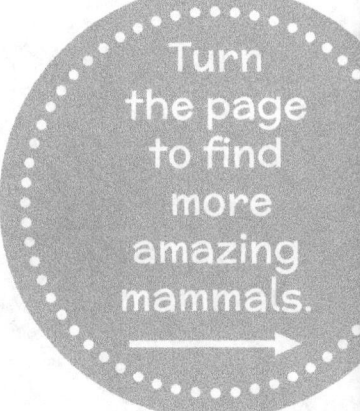

Turn the page to find more amazing mammals.

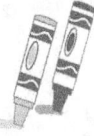 *Trace and color this running cheetah.*

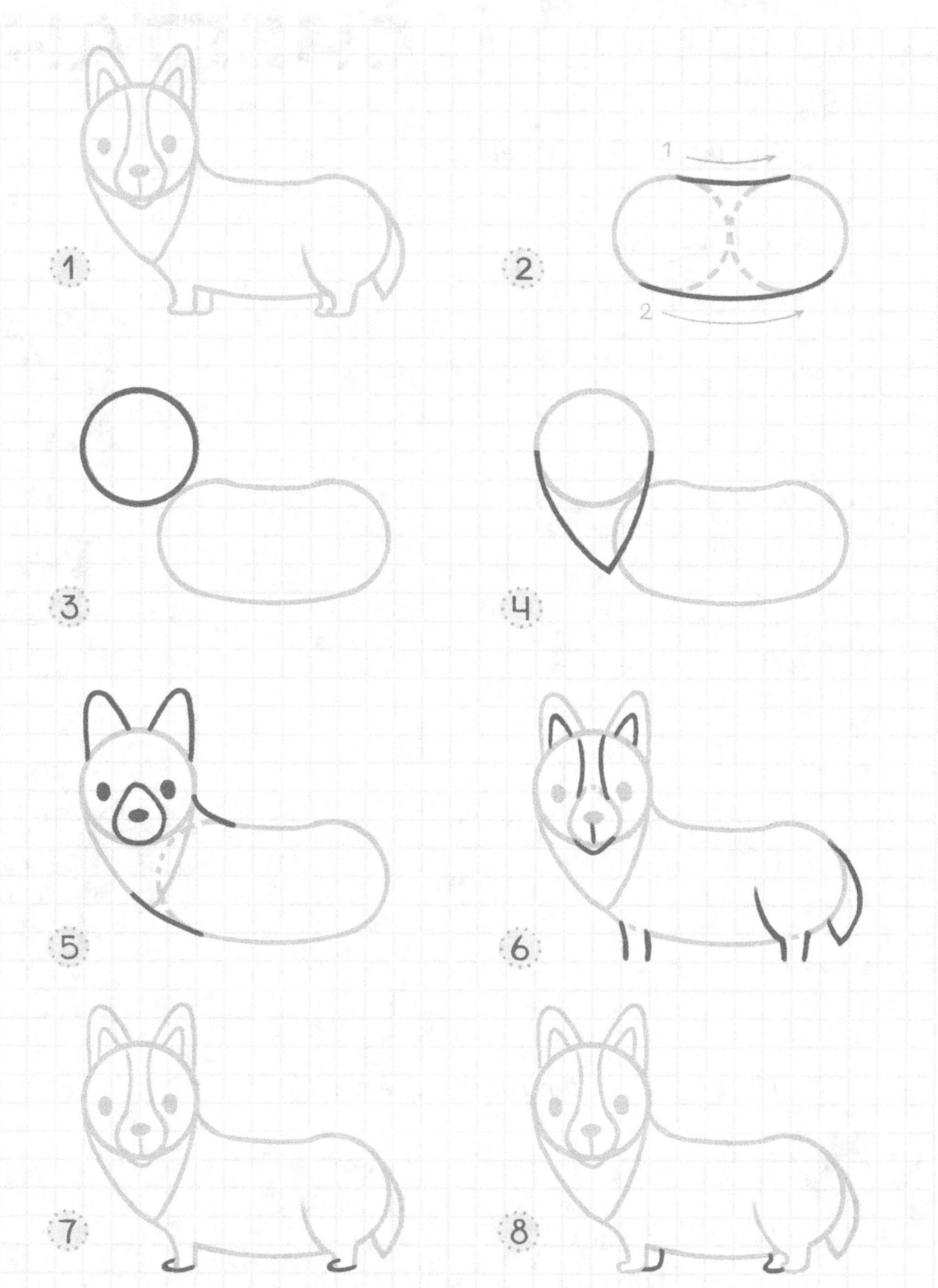

1

2

3

4

5

6

7

8

Animals by Alisa Bloom | Draw & Learn™ Book Series

DOG

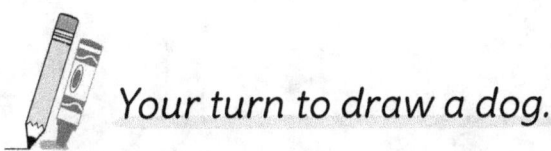
Your turn to draw a dog.

Dogs are wonderful pets—they're friendly and lots of fun. **Puppies**, or baby dogs, make great playmates and love chasing after toys. Dogs come in many shapes and sizes, from small French Bulldogs with short hair to big Golden Retrievers with fluffy coats. Different types of dogs are called breeds .

This is a corgi. It has a bushy tail, big brown eyes, short legs, and large pointy ears. ▶

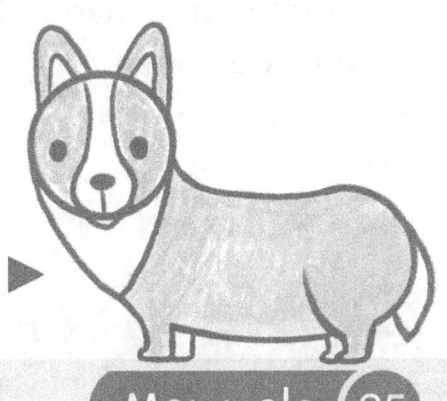

1

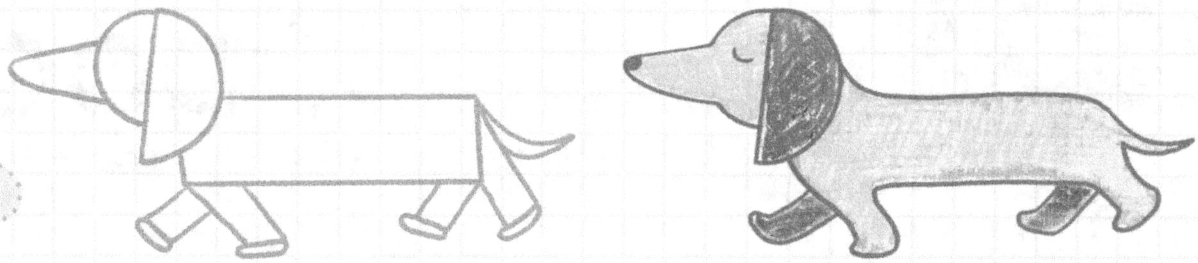

2

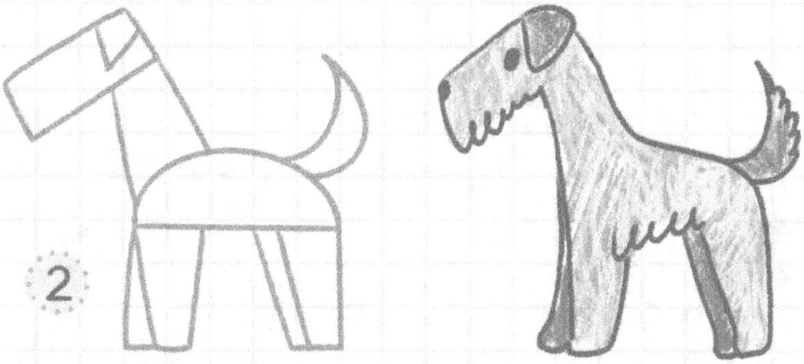

Dachshunds, often called
sausage dogs, have short
legs and long bodies.

Terriers have rough,
ragged coats and
fluffy tails that curl up.

3

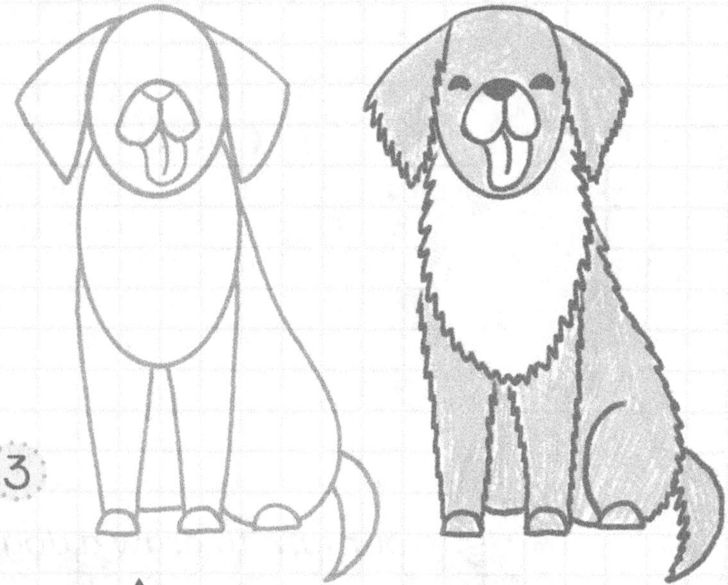

4

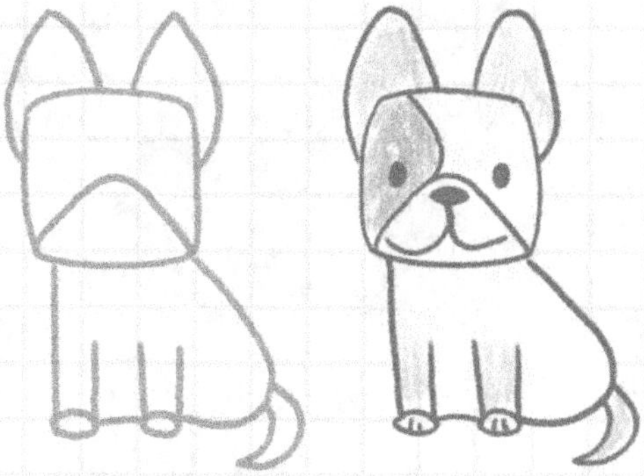

French Bulldogs have
square-shaped heads
and large, bat-like ears.

Golden Retrievers
have smiling faces,
floppy ears, and
beautiful coats.

Dalmatians have
spotted coats.

5

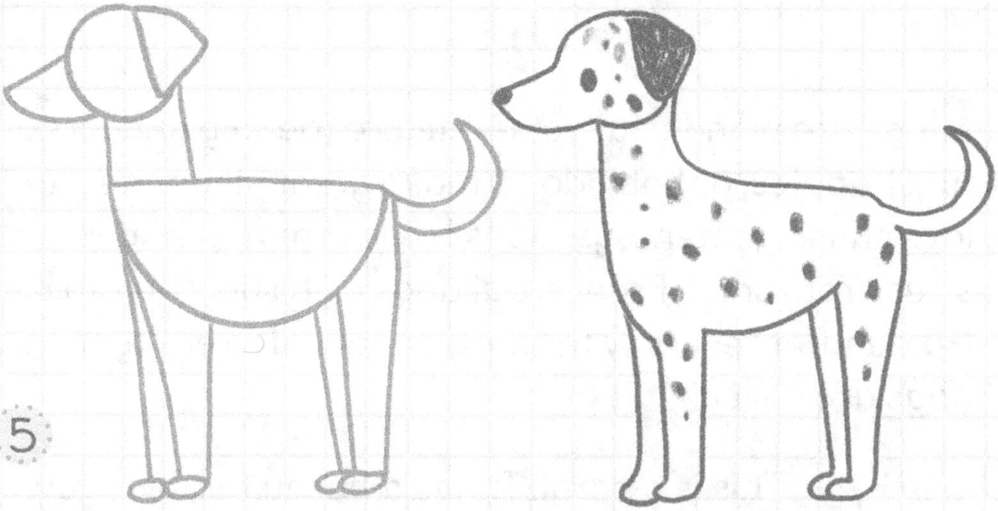

 Find the shapes used to draw these dogs.

1

2

3

4

5

Finish drawing the dogs on this page by using simple shapes.

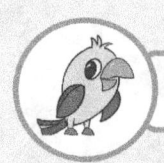 Do you think dogs and wolves are cousins?

Wolves and dogs are cousins because they both belong to the same family—canines. While most dogs live with people as pets, wolves are wild animals that roam forests and grasslands. Like dogs, wolves can bark, but they also howl—their howl can be heard from miles away! These social animals live in groups called **packs**, where they play, hunt, and protect their home together. In a pack, everyone helps care for baby wolves, known as **pups**.

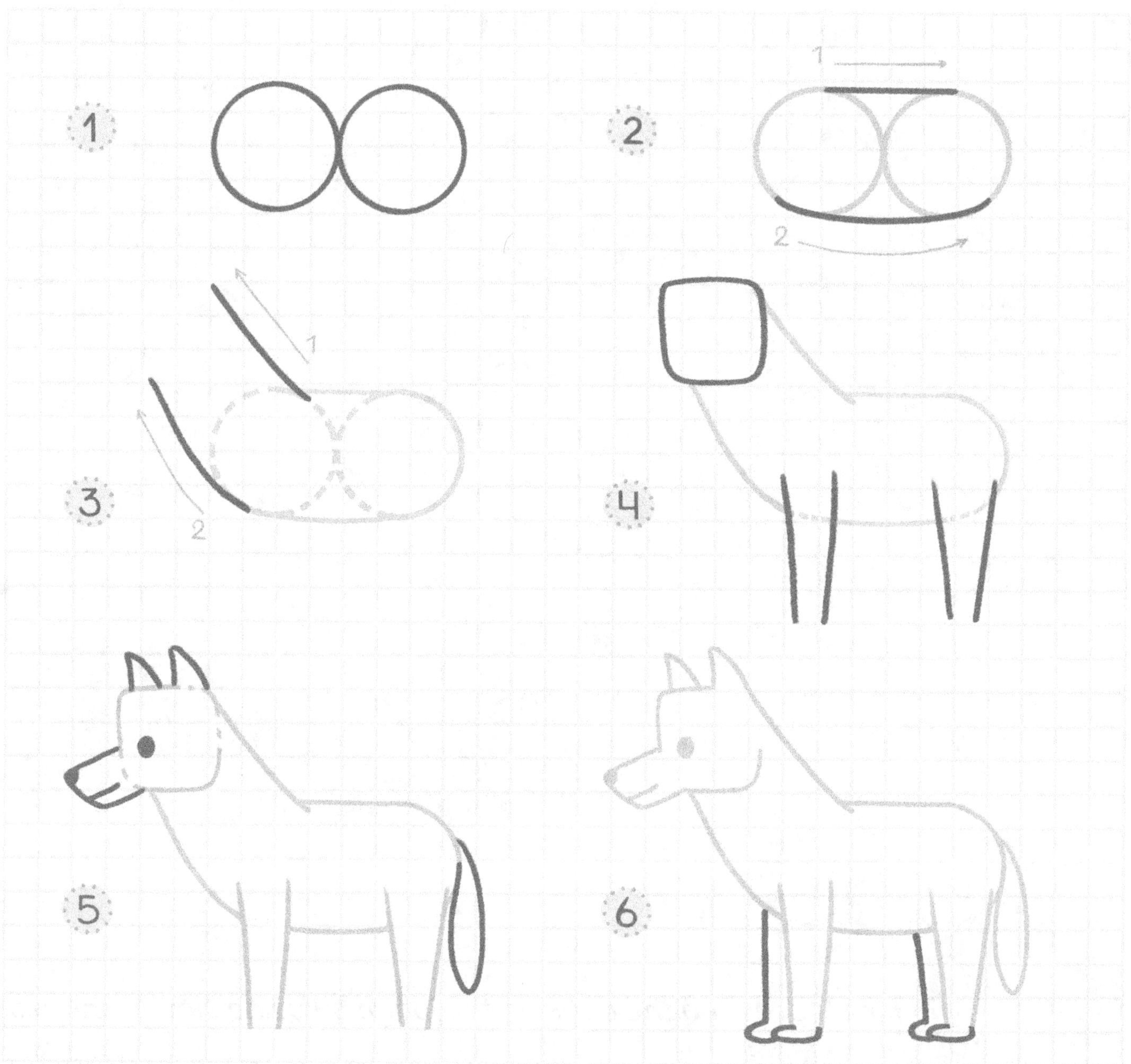

WOLF

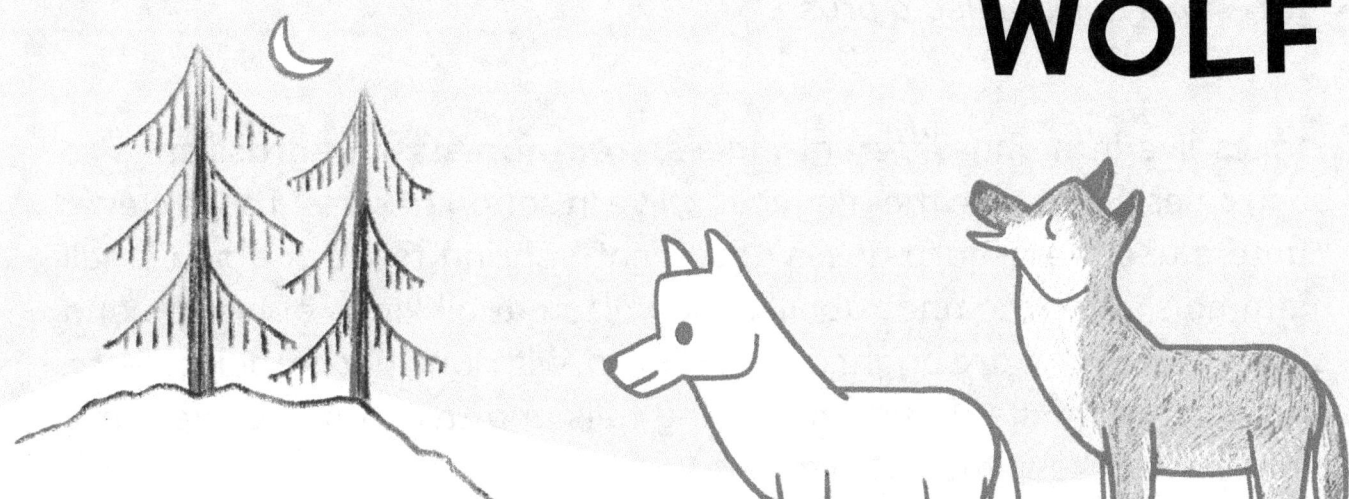

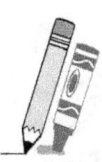 *Your turn to draw wolves.*

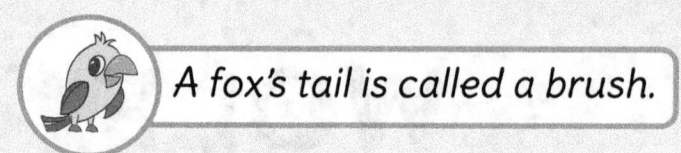

A fox's tail is called a brush.

Foxes live in many different places, from forests and grasslands to busy cities. Some, like the fennec fox, live in sandy deserts. These clever hunters use their sharp noses and great hearing to track down small mammals, like mice and rabbits. They also eat all kinds of insects and plants. Most foxes are bright orange or red, with long heads, pointy ears, and narrow snouts. Their long, bushy tails and thick fur are like fluffy blankets that keep them warm.

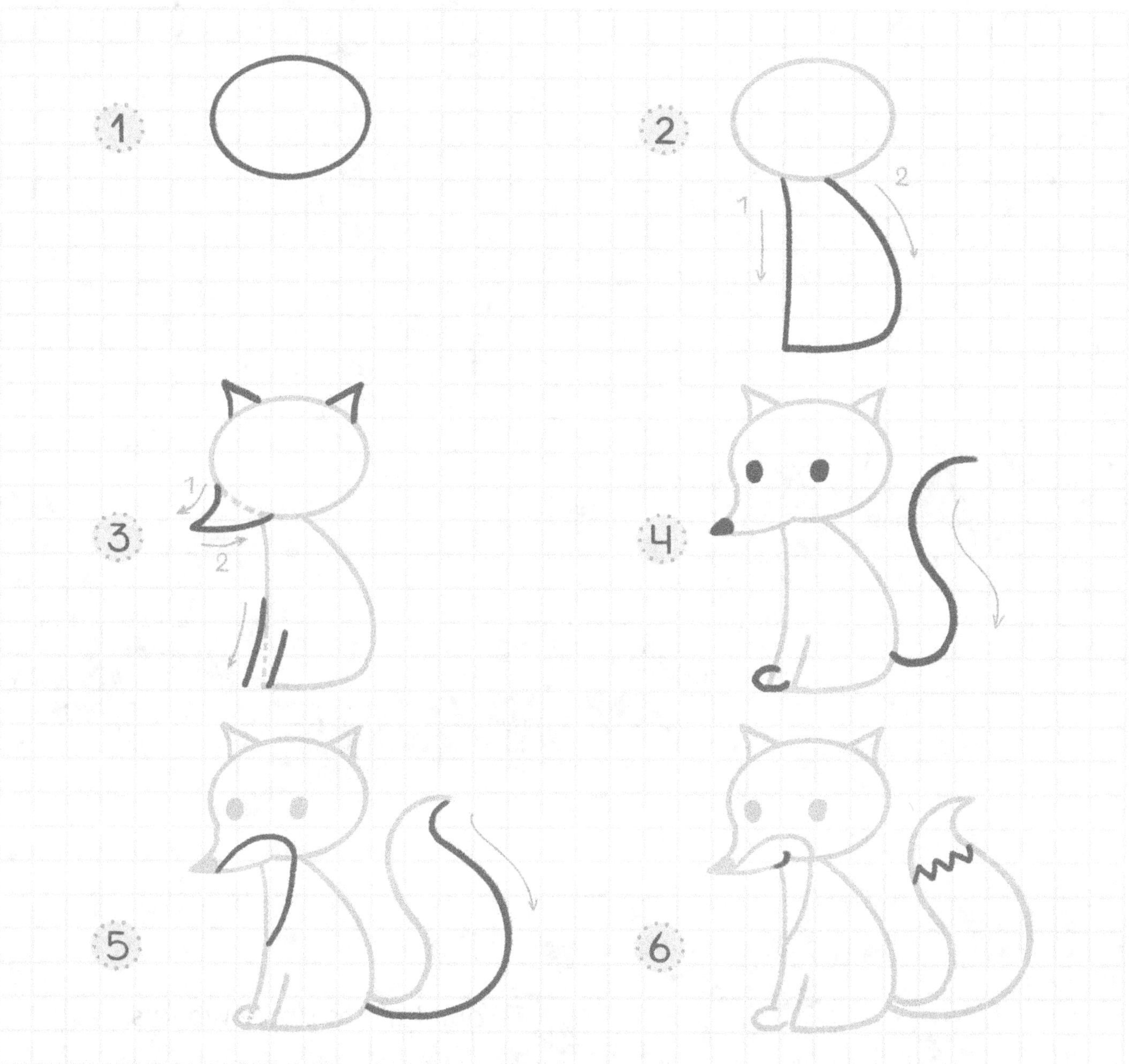

1

2

3

4

5

6

FOX

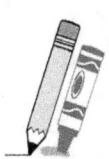 *Your turn to draw foxes.*

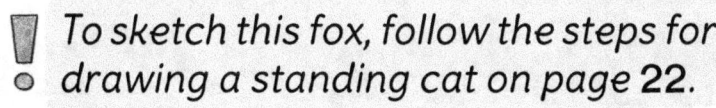 *To sketch this fox, follow the steps for drawing a standing cat on page 22.*

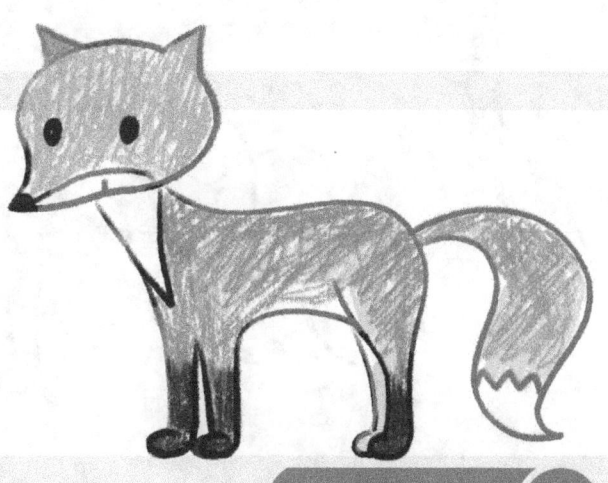

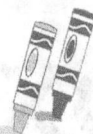 *Draw more trees to create a forest and color this picture.*

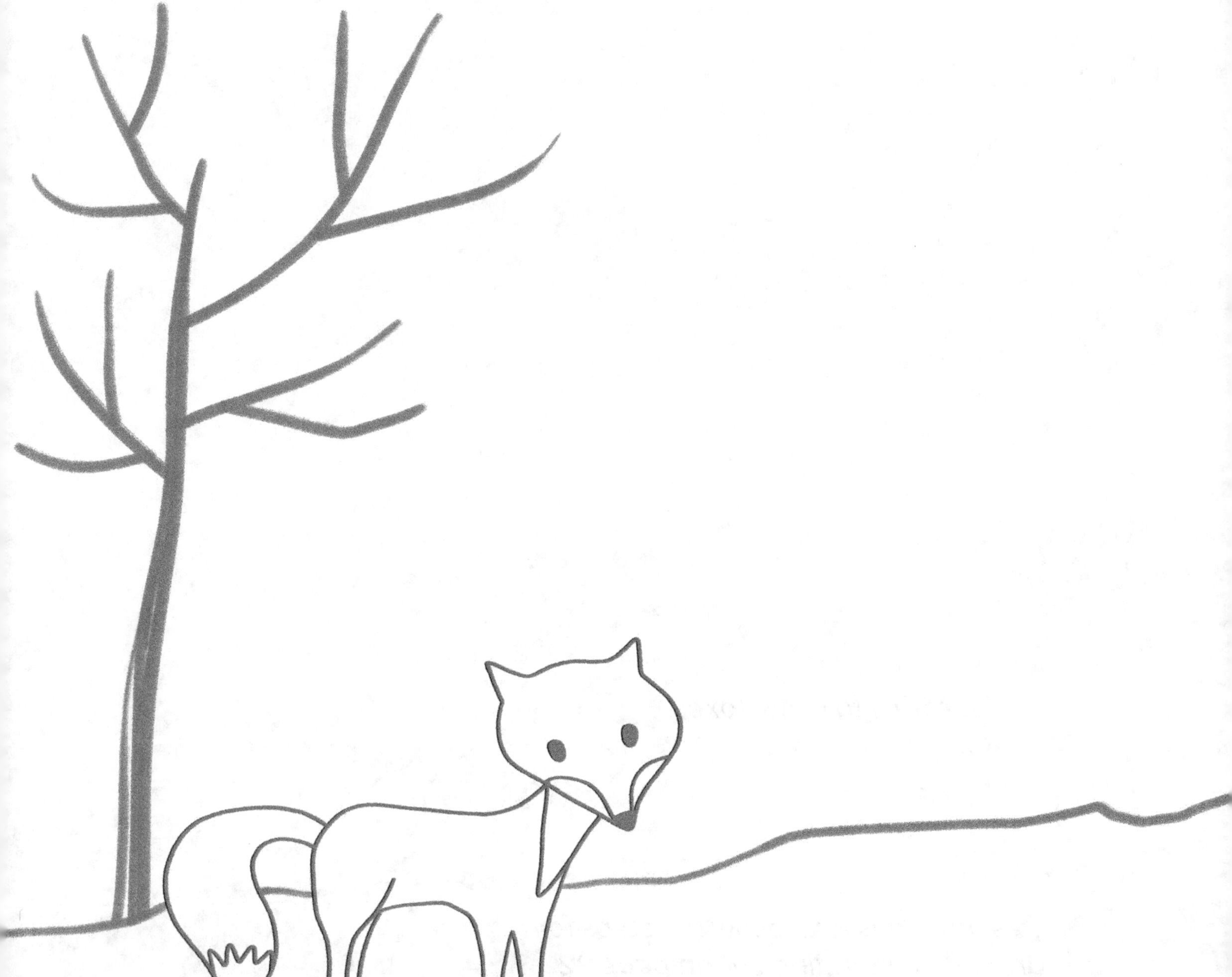

Animals by Alisa Bloom | Draw & Learn™ Book Series

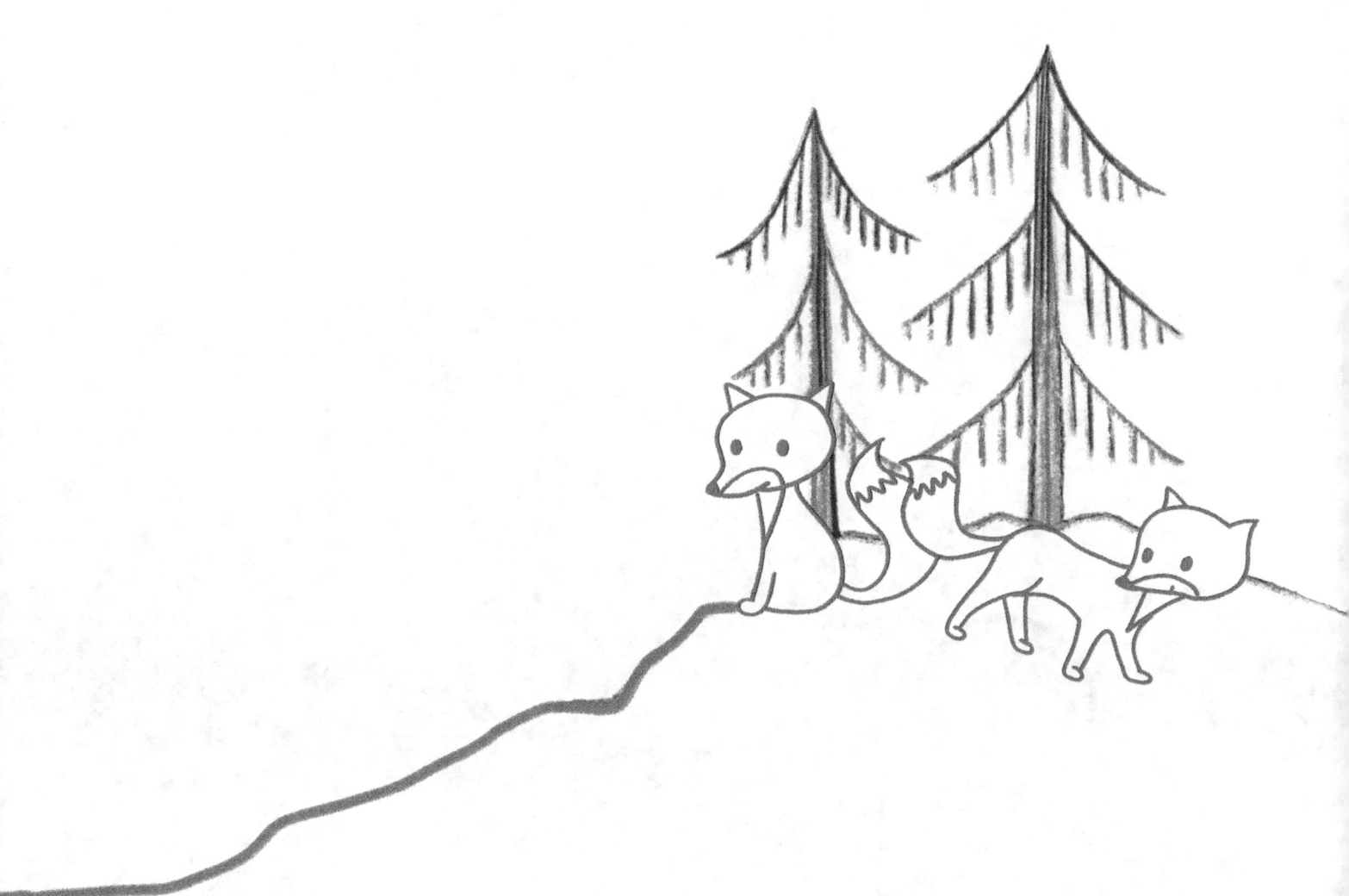

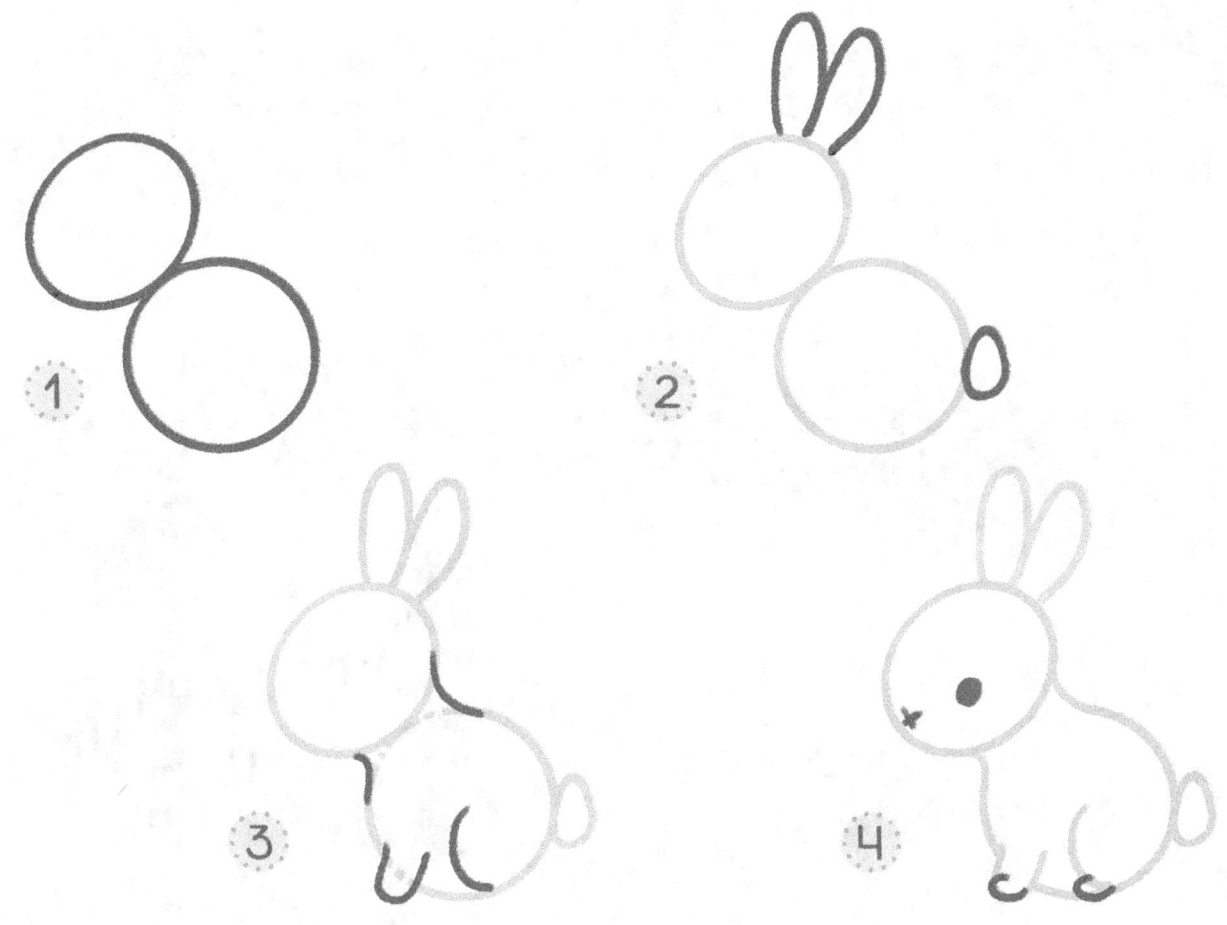

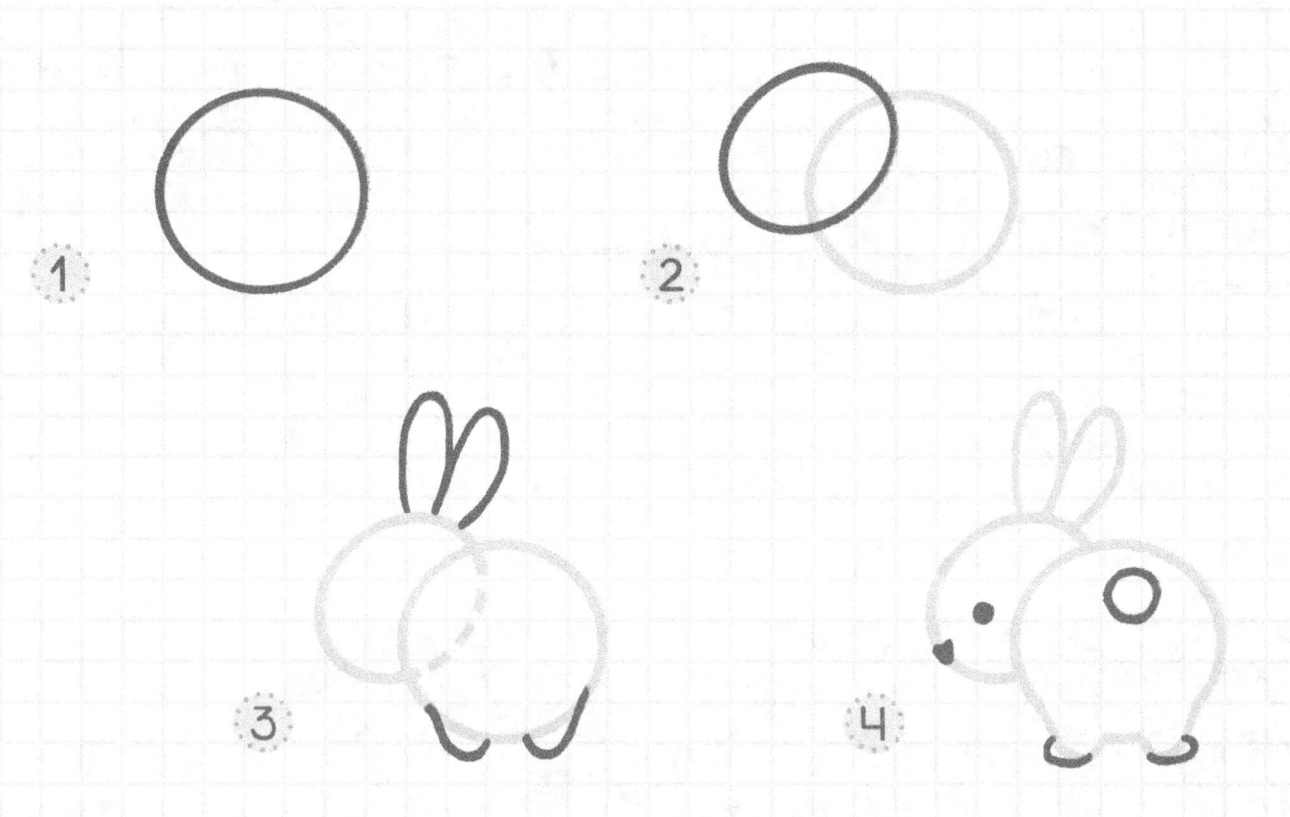

Animals by Alisa Bloom | Draw & Learn™ Book Series

RABBIT

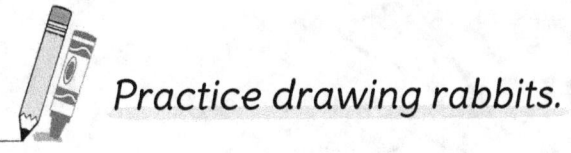
Practice drawing rabbits.

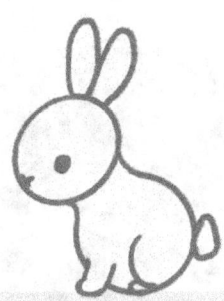

Rabbits, also called **bunnies**, are small, fluffy animals with round faces and bright eyes. Their fur can be brown, gray, white, or patterned. Most rabbits have ears that stand up, while some, like lop-eared rabbits, have floppy ears that hang down. A rabbit's ears can turn almost all the way around! You can find these lively animals hopping around in forests and grasslands. Some even live in deserts. Many make their homes in long underground tunnels called burrows. As herbivores, rabbits eat plants like grass, flowers, and leafy greens.

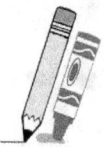 *Draw tall flowers to help the two little bunnies hide from the fox.*

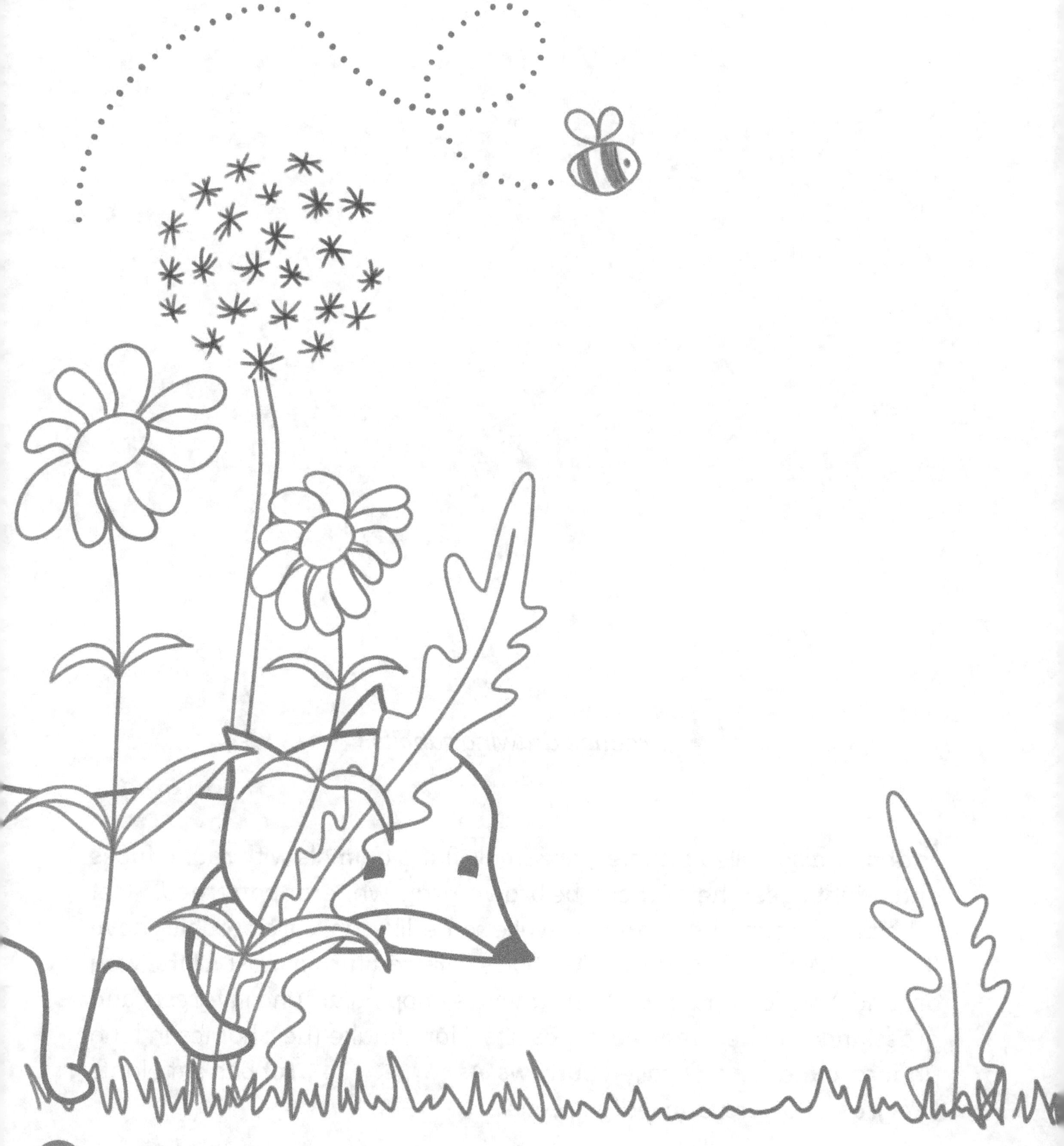

Animals by Alisa Bloom | Draw & Learn™ Book Series

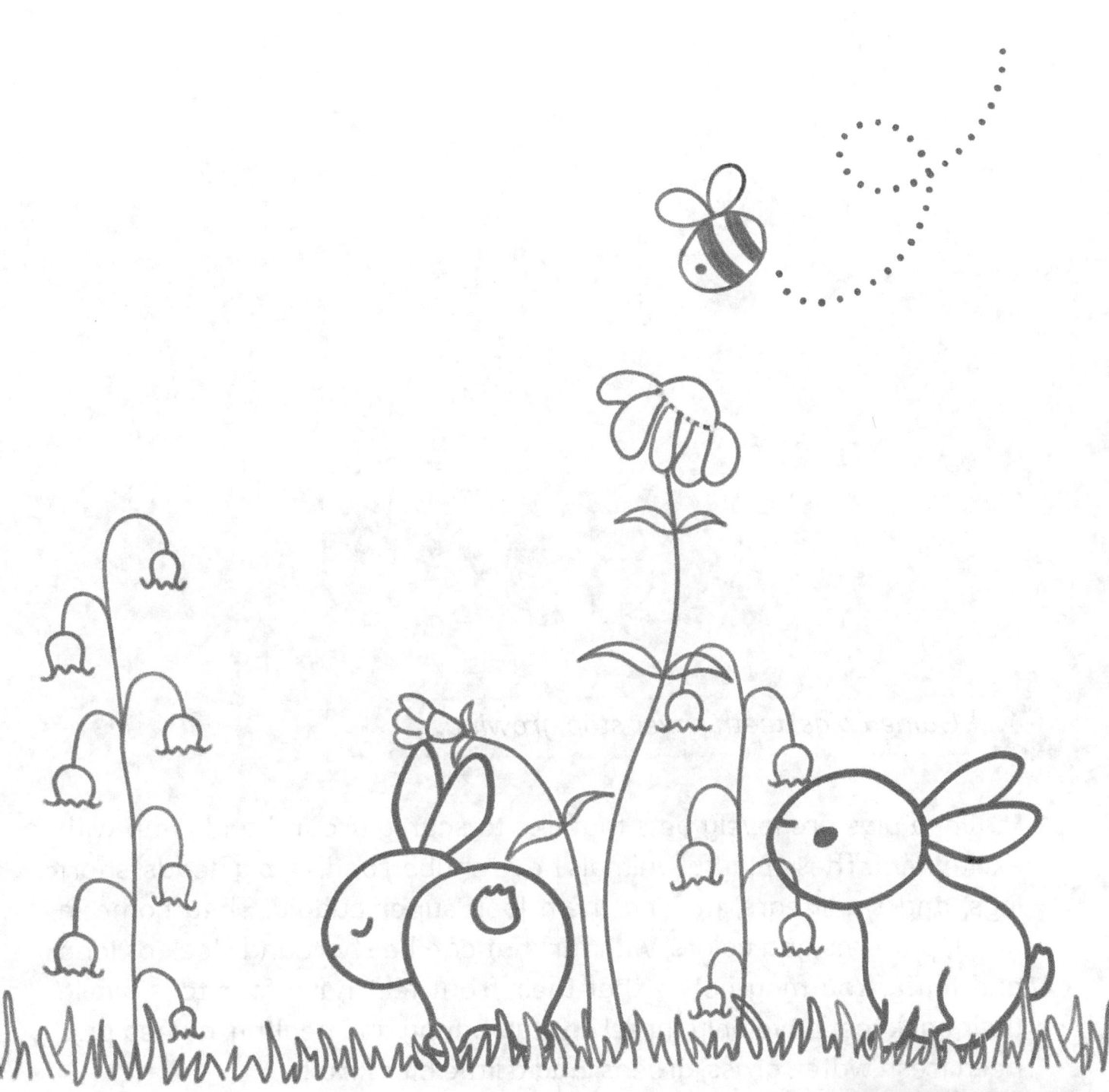

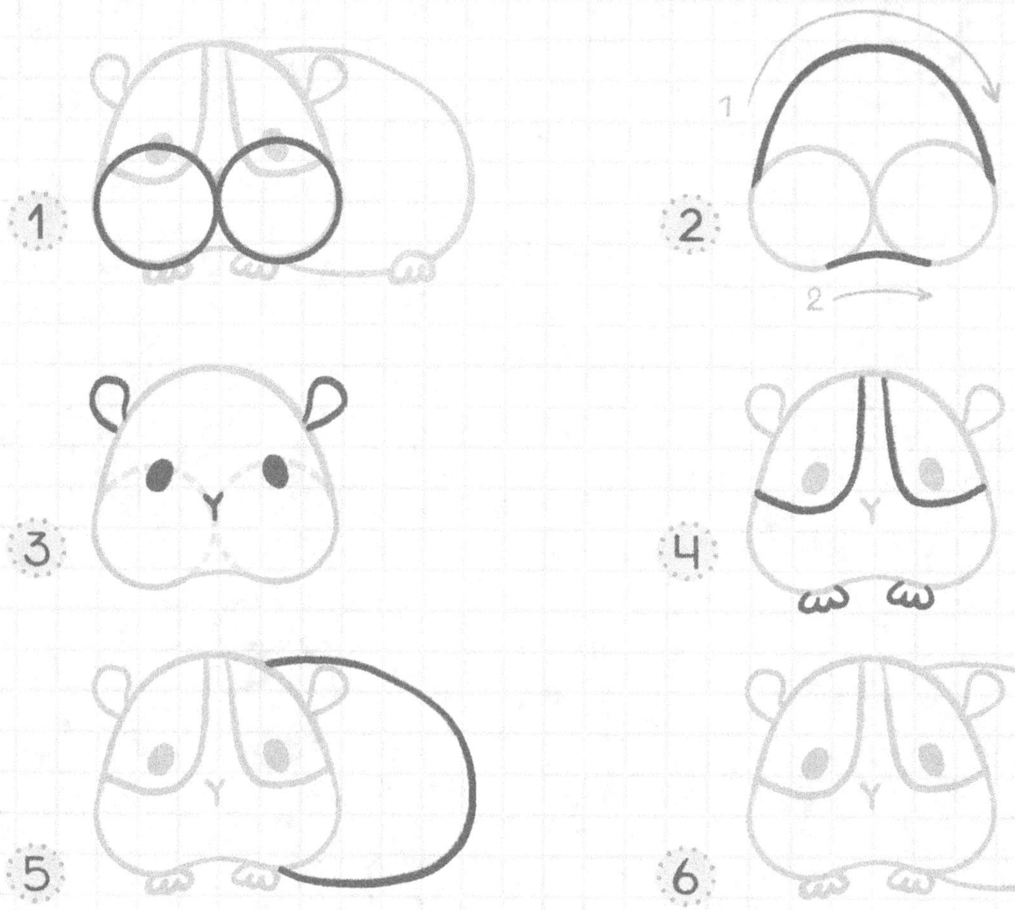

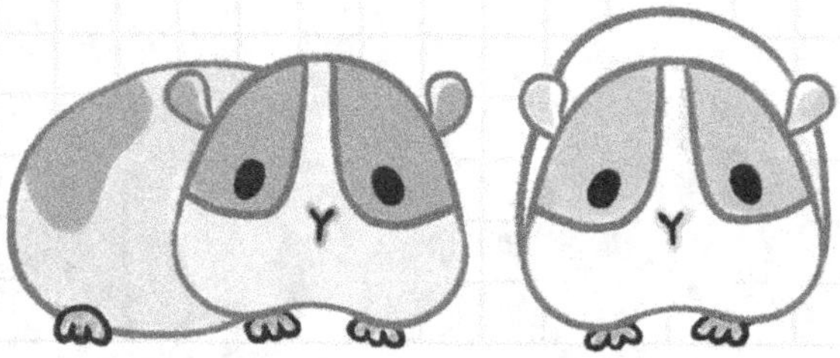

1

2

3

4

5

6

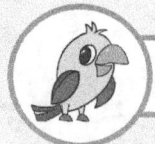 *Guinea pigs' teeth never stop growing.*

Guinea pigs are lovely pets that like to scurry around and jump with excitement. These playful animals have chubby bodies, big heads, short legs, and small ears, making them look super cuddly. They come in many patterns and colors, with fur that can be short and sleek or long and fluffy. You may notice that their front feet have four toes, while their back feet have only three! To stay happy and healthy, guinea pigs need fresh water, grass, greens, and a little bit of fruit.

Animals by Alisa Bloom | Draw & Learn™ Book Series

GUINEA PIG

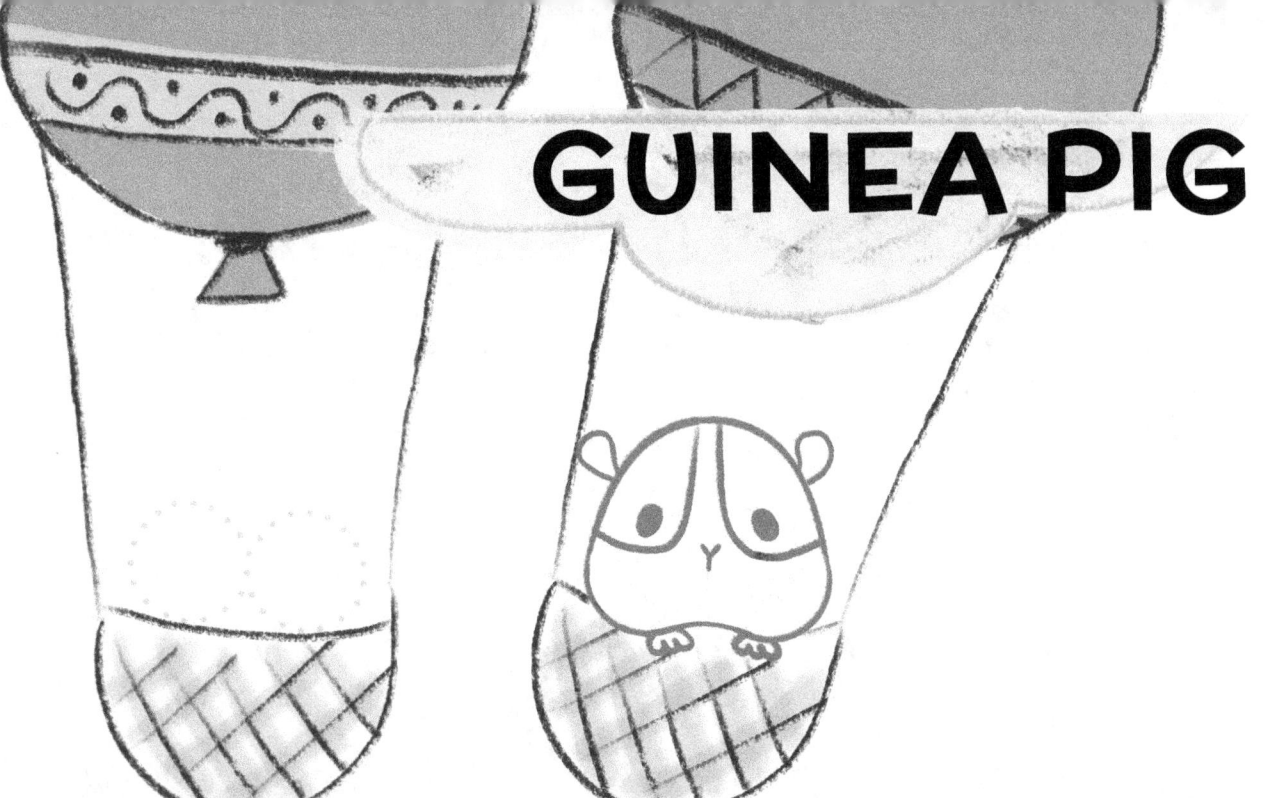

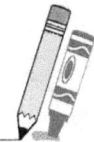 *Your turn to draw guinea pigs.*

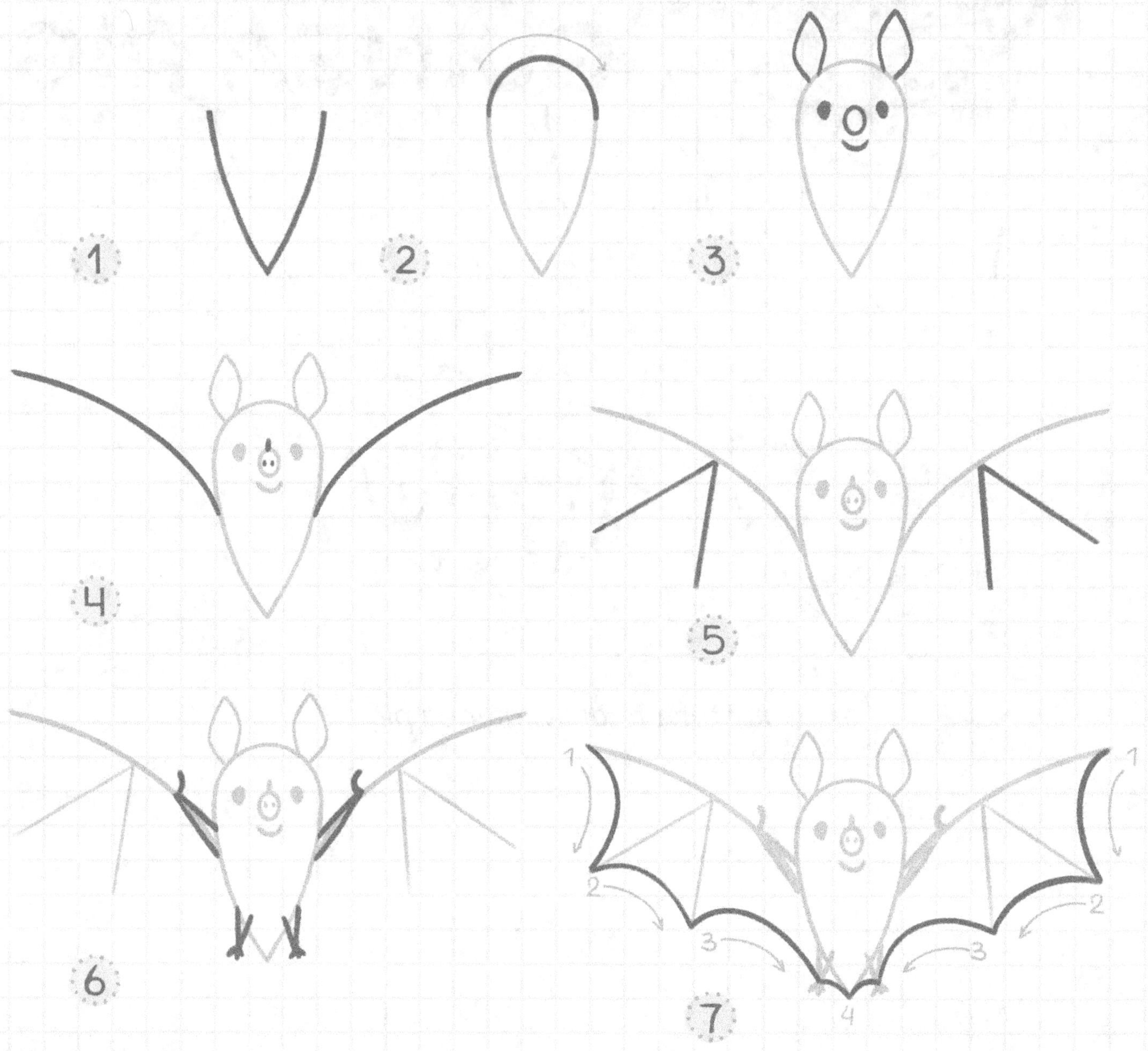

1

2

3

4

5

6

7

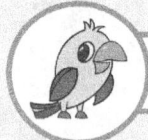 *Some bats can eat hundreds of mosquitoes in just one hour!*

Bats are the only mammals that can fly. Some have wings as wide as a human's arm span, while others are as small as a strawberry. Baby bats learn to fly when they're young. They have soft fur that keeps them warm and can be black, brown, or gray. Bats live in large groups called **colonies.** They're often found in caves, hollow trees, old buildings, and under bridges. At night, bats hunt for bugs and fruit. During the day, they sleep upside down with their wings wrapped around them.

Animals by Alisa Bloom | Draw & Learn™ Book Series

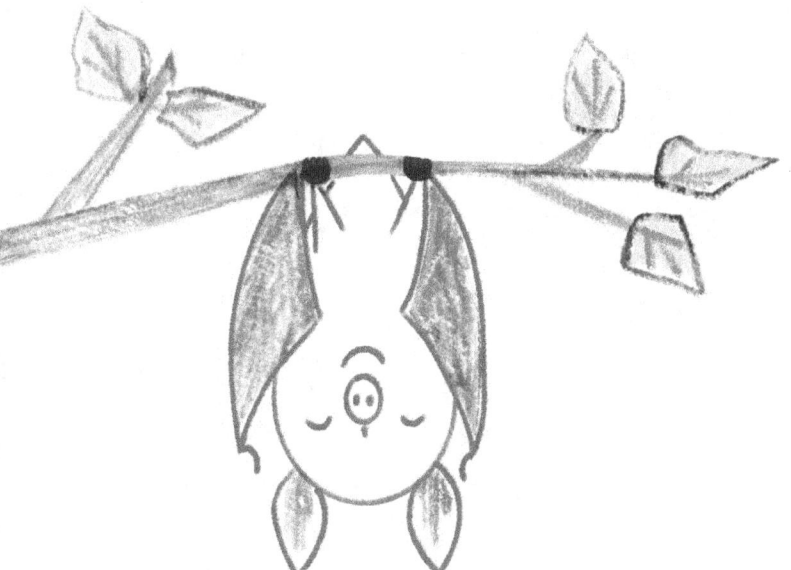

BAT

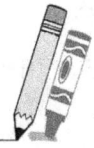 *Draw a bat. Start by tracing the shape above.*

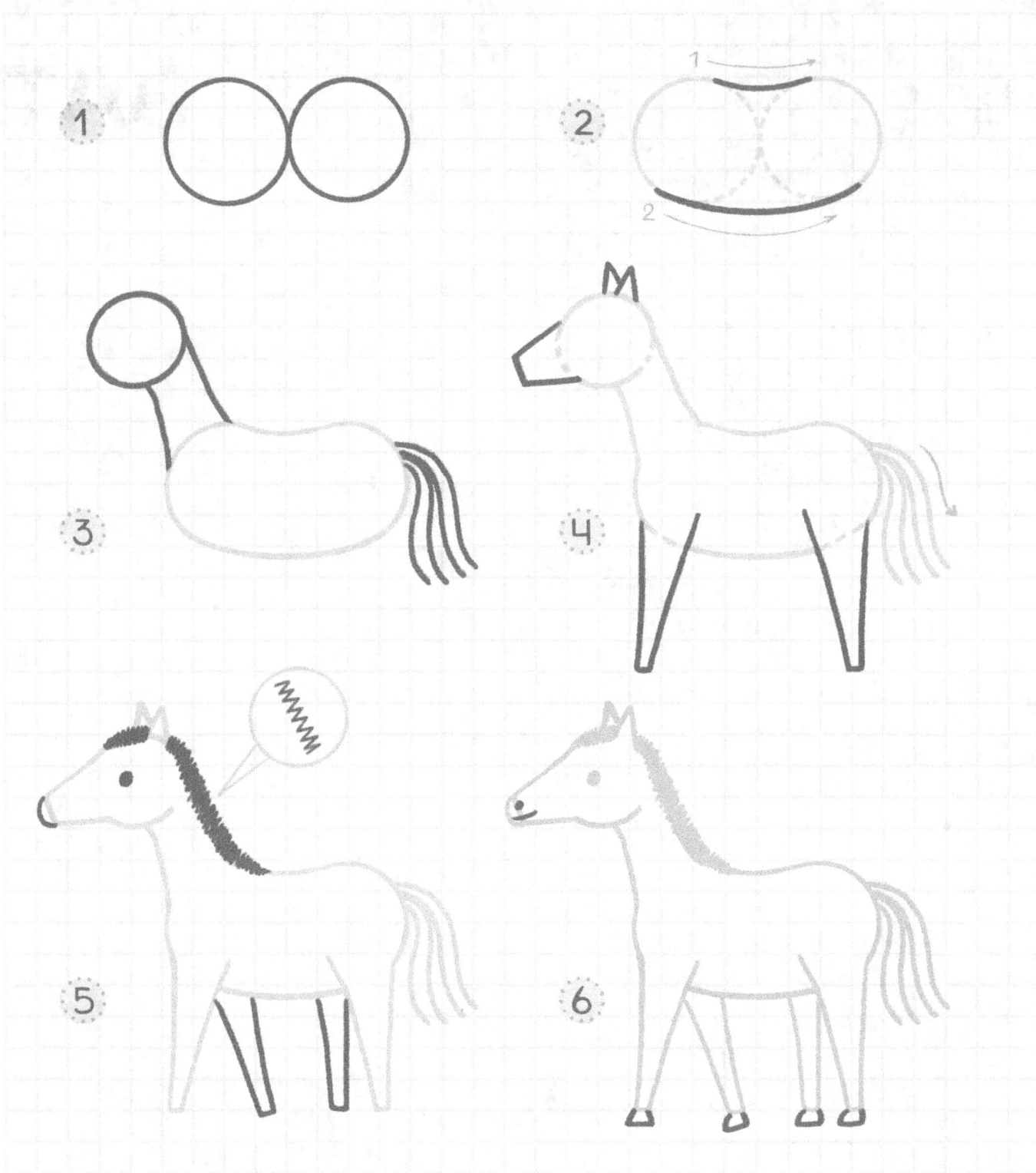

Ponies are like little horses. They're friendly and great for kids to ride. Even though they're smaller, ponies are just as strong and can carry heavy loads. Ponies have one big toe on each foot, covered by a hard hoof. Baby ponies, called **foals**, love to run and play. Just hours after they're born, they can already walk! Foals drink their mom's milk and eat treats like apples and carrots once their teeth grow in.

PONY

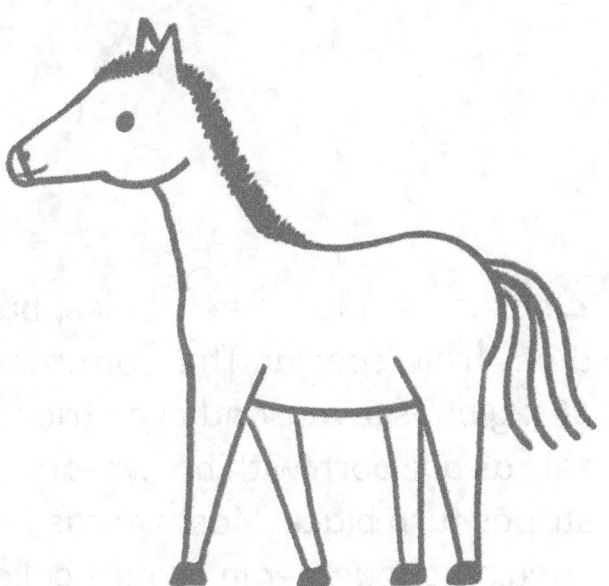

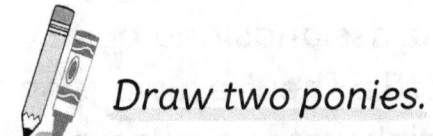
Draw two ponies.

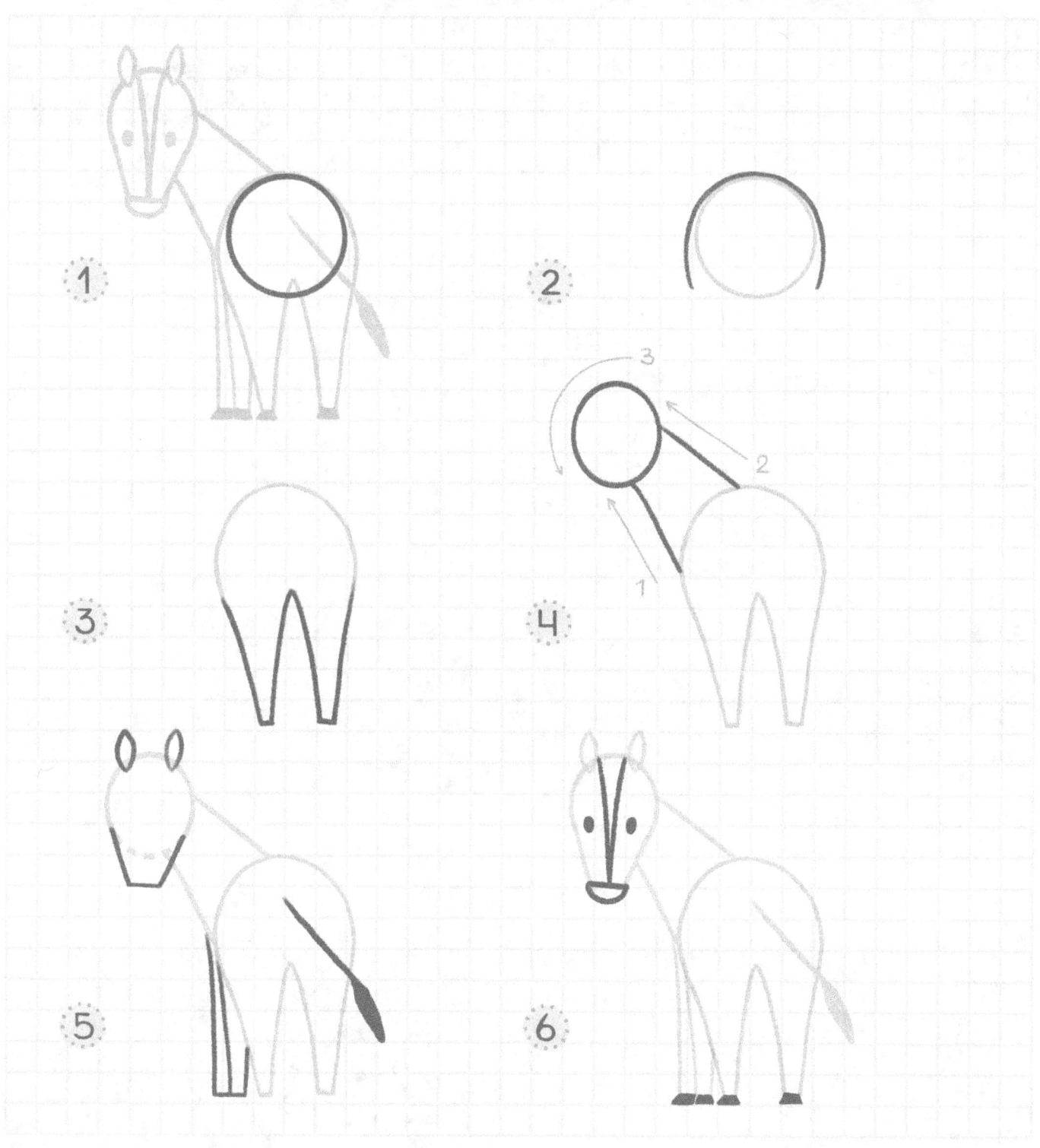

1

2

3

4

5

6

Zebras may look like horses, but their black-and-white stripes make them truly special. Their amazing patterns help them stay cool, keep pesky bugs away, and even trick sneaky predators. Did you know baby zebras are born with brown-and-white stripes? As they grow older, the stripes turn black. Most zebras live in grasslands and open woodlands. They stay together in groups called **herds**. They're always on the move, looking for the perfect place to rest, drink water, and graze on grass.

ZEBRA

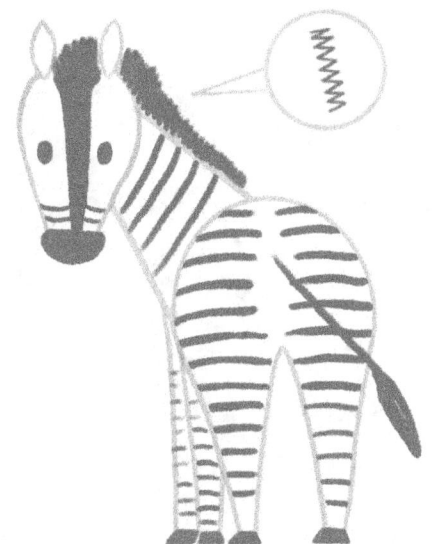

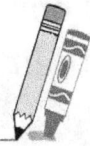 *How many zebras can you draw on this page?*

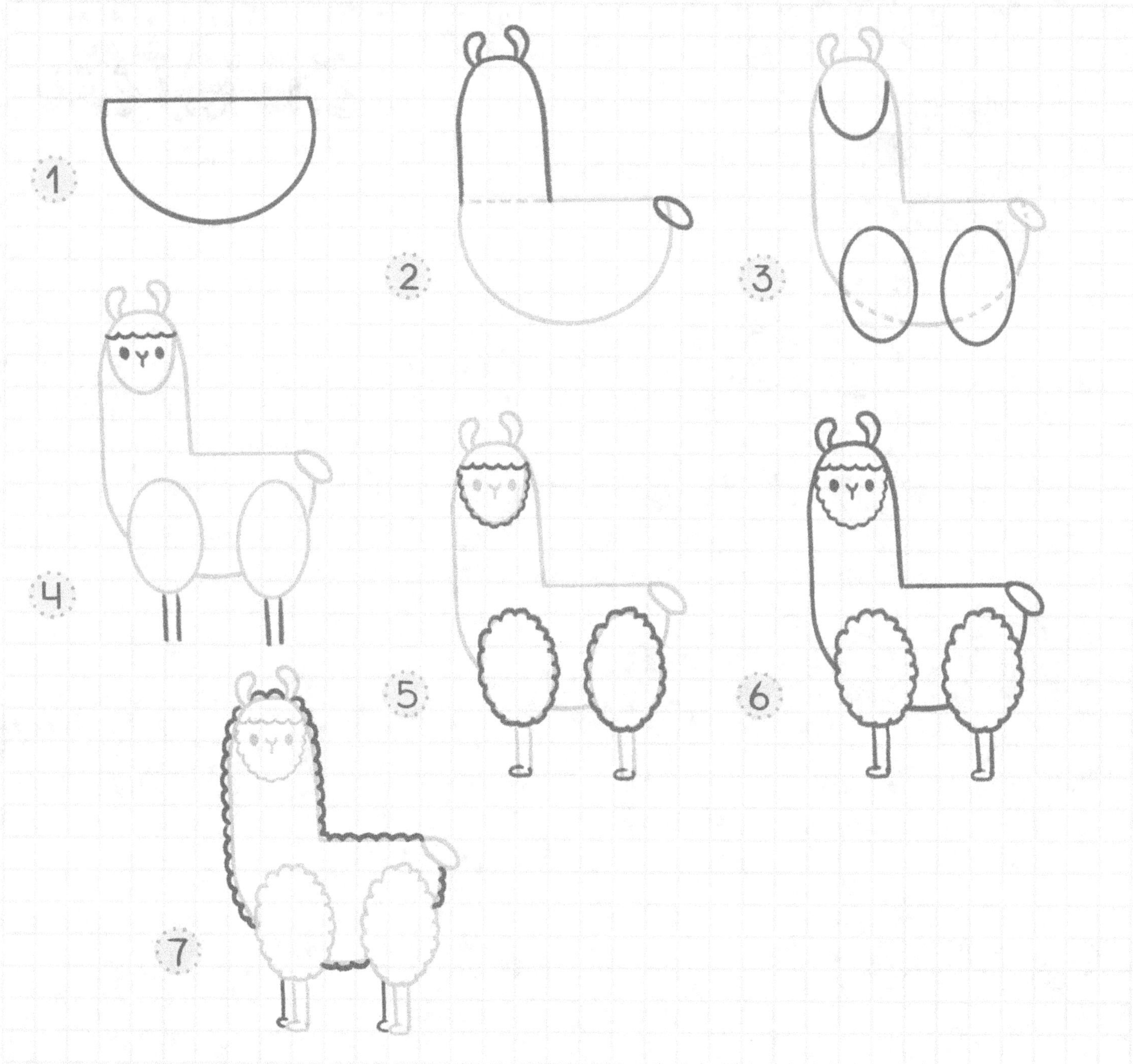

1

2

3

4

5

6

7

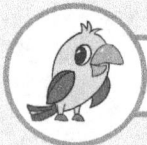 *A young llama is called a **cria**, which means "baby" in Spanish.*

Llamas used to live in the wild, but now they're mostly found on farms. These friendly animals help keep goats and sheep safe from coyotes and other predators. With their long necks, small heads, skinny legs, and short tails, llamas are easy to spot. Their banana-shaped ears and woolly coats, which can be black, brown, red, or white, make them look even cuter. Llamas love nibbling on grass, leaves, and twigs.

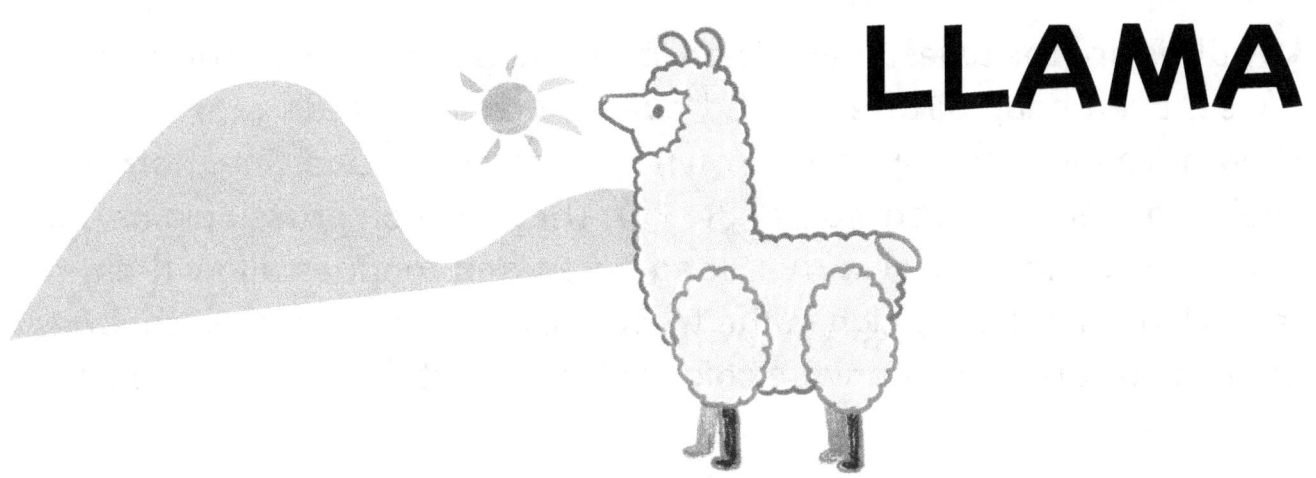

LLAMA

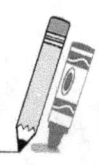 *Draw a llama in the mountains.*

Giraffes are the tallest animals on land—they can grow as tall as a big house! Even baby giraffes, called **calves**, are taller than most people. They have long legs, spotted brown-orange coats, and tiny, horn-like knobs on their heads called ossicones. They walk on grassy plains and rest in the shade of trees. Their long necks and tongues allow them to reach leaves and fruit high in the treetops. Did you know their tongues are bluish-purple? This unique color helps protect them from sunburn.

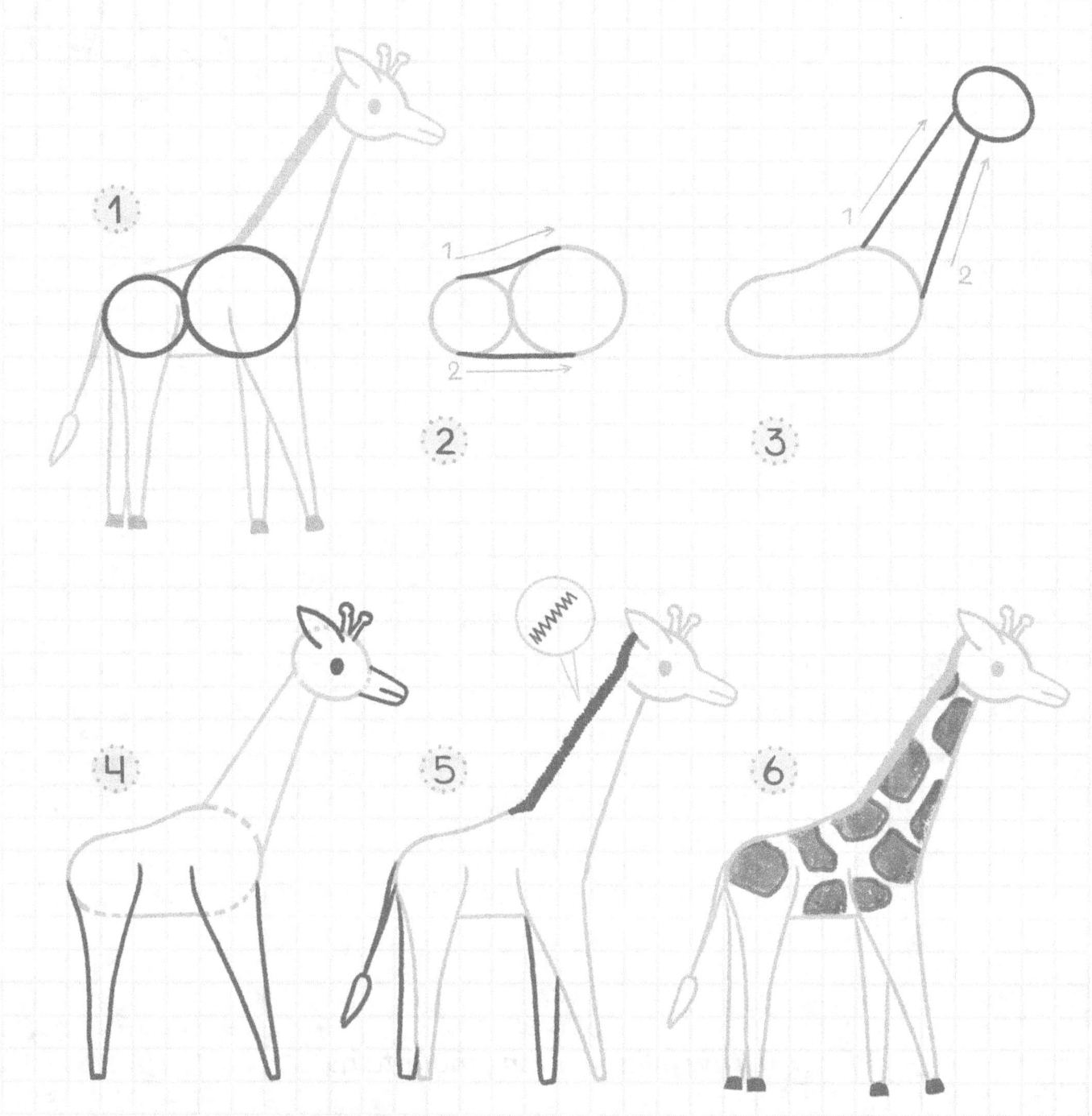

Animals by Alisa Bloom | Draw & Learn™ Book Series

GIRAFFE

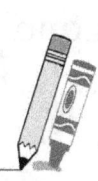 *Draw a tall giraffe and a calf.*

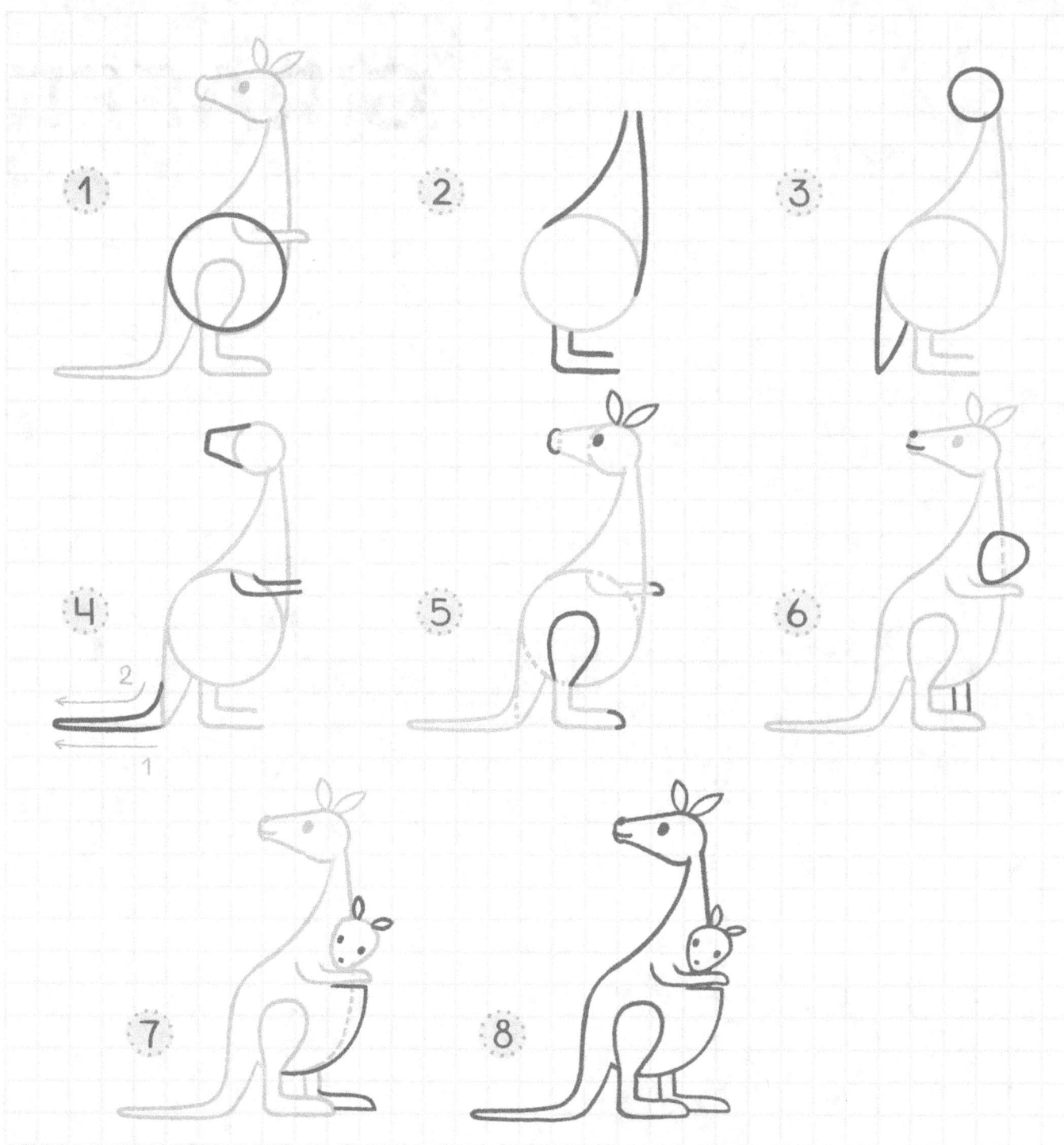

Kangaroos are part of a special group of mammals with pouches, called marsupials. They carry their babies, known as **joeys**, in a soft pouch on their tummy—how cozy! Kangaroos have big ears, dark eyes, and strong bodies with short gray or red-brown fur. They don't run like most animals. Instead, they hop using their hind legs and balance with their tails. They live in open woodlands and grasslands, eating plants and sometimes going without water for days.

KANGAROO

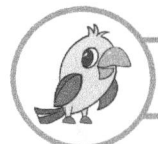 How many marsupials can you name?

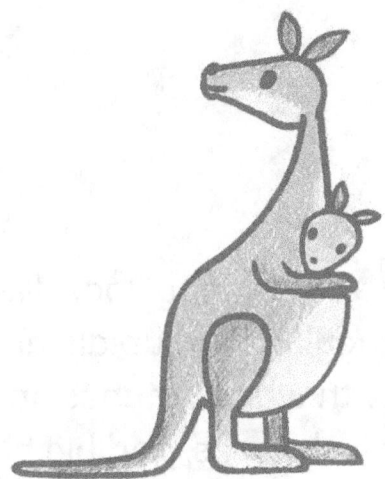

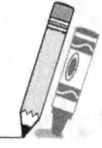 Draw two mommy kangaroos with their joeys.

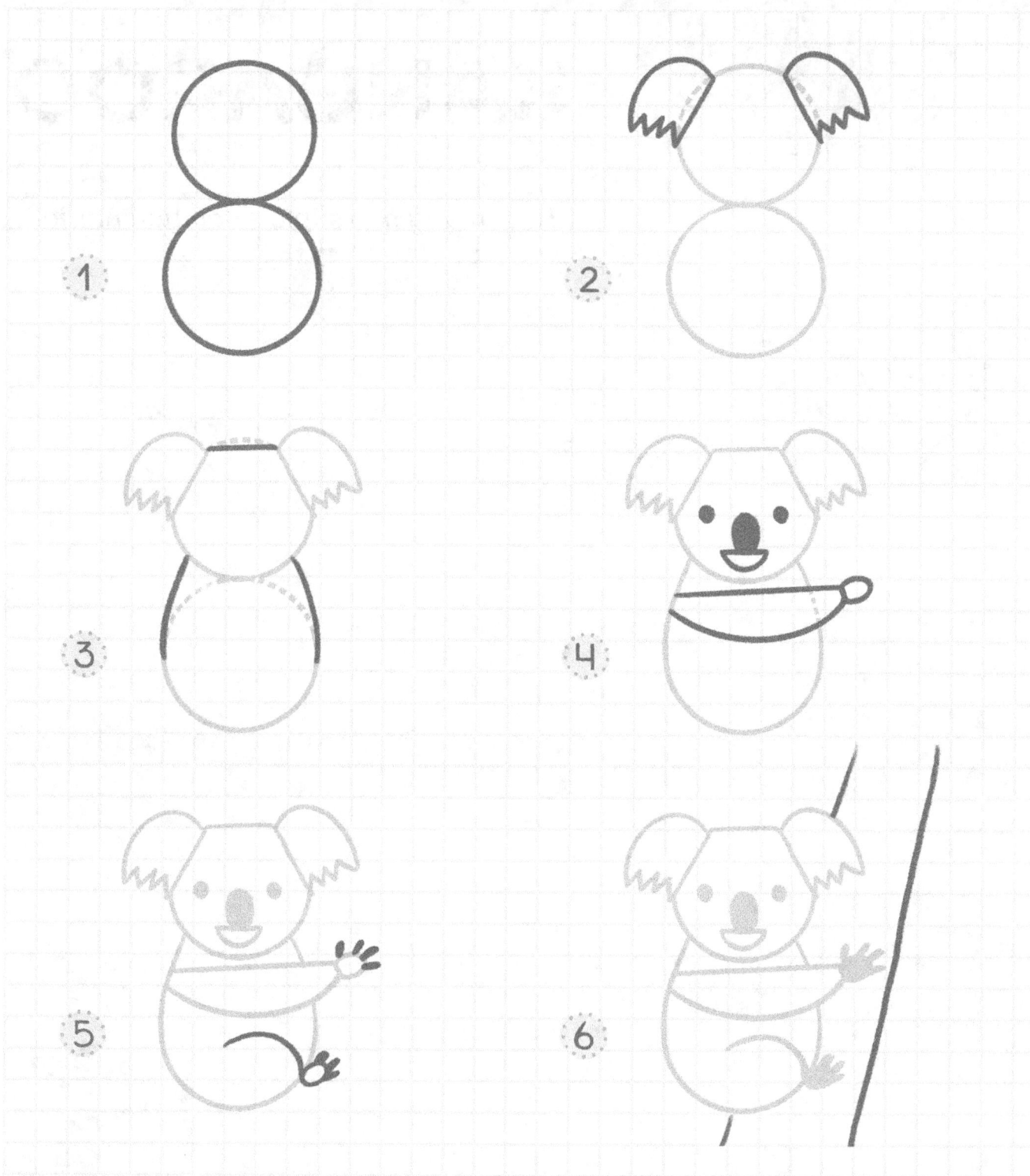

1

2

3

4

5

6

Koalas may look like small bears, but they're not! Like kangaroos, they're marsupials and carry their babies in pouches. Their fur is gray with white patches on their chests and inside their ears. With furry ears, plush coats, and big black noses, koalas look so soft and huggable. They love eating eucalyptus leaves more than anything else. Most of the time, they climb and nap in their favorite trees, like true nap champions.

KOALA

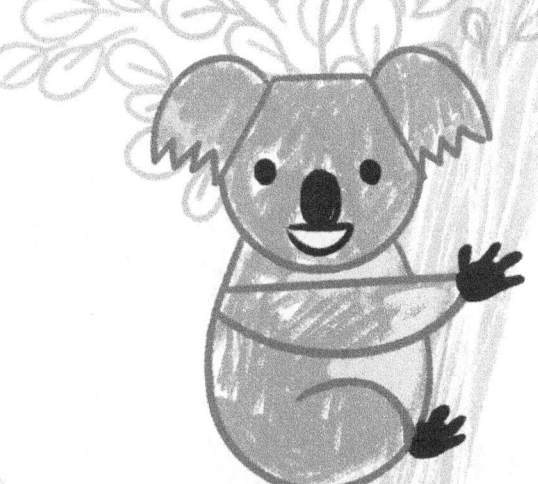

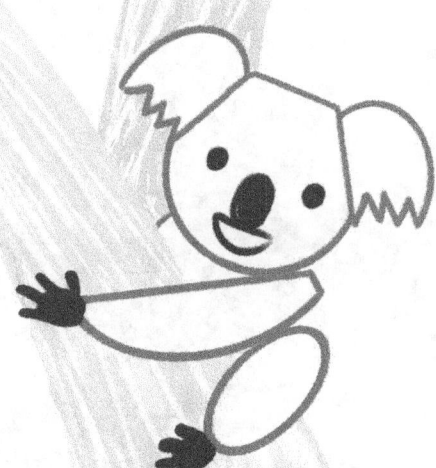

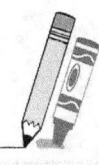 Draw a koala hanging from the tree above.

Follow the steps to draw furry koala ears...

1   2   3

... and paws.

1   2

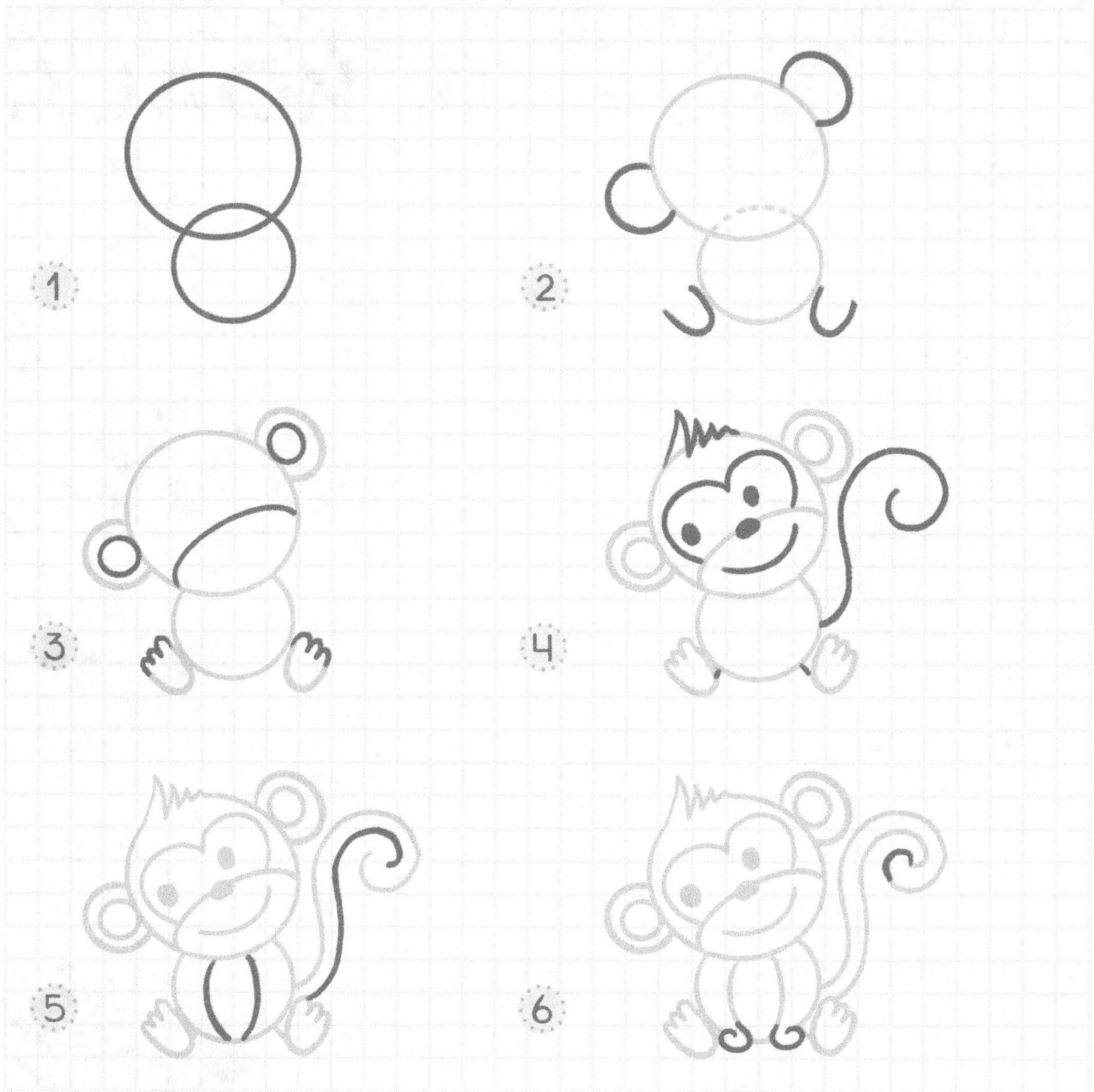

1

2

3

4

5

6

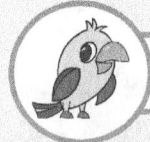 *Monkeys "talk" to each other by making sounds and funny faces.*

Monkeys are fun to watch. They're clever and can use tools like sticks and rocks. Monkeys live in groups called **troops**. They're often found in rainforests with plenty of fruit, like figs and bananas. Some stay on the ground, while others swing from tree to tree like acrobats. Their babies, called **infants**, are curious and learn quickly by copying older monkeys. Their furry bodies can be black, brown, red, yellow, or even blue.

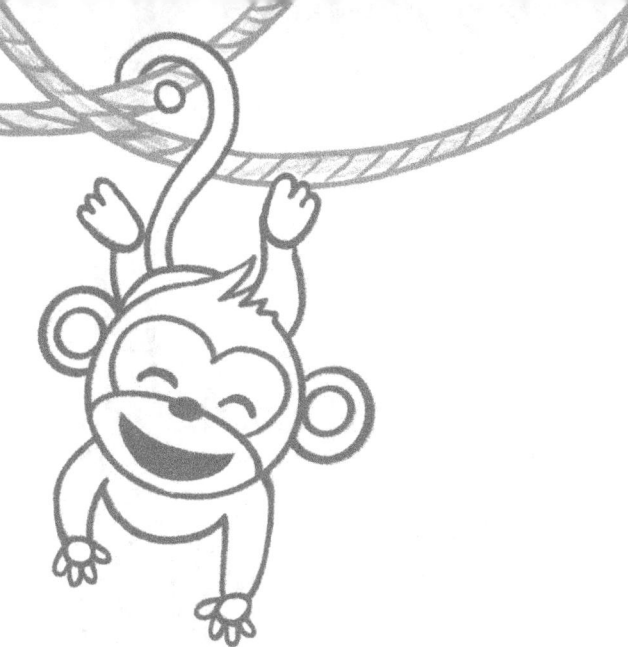

MONKEY

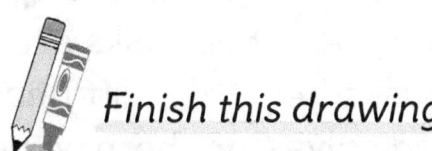

Finish this drawing.

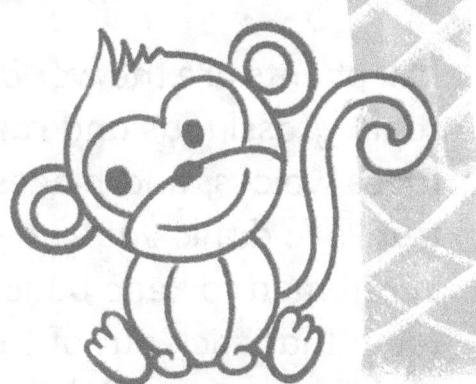

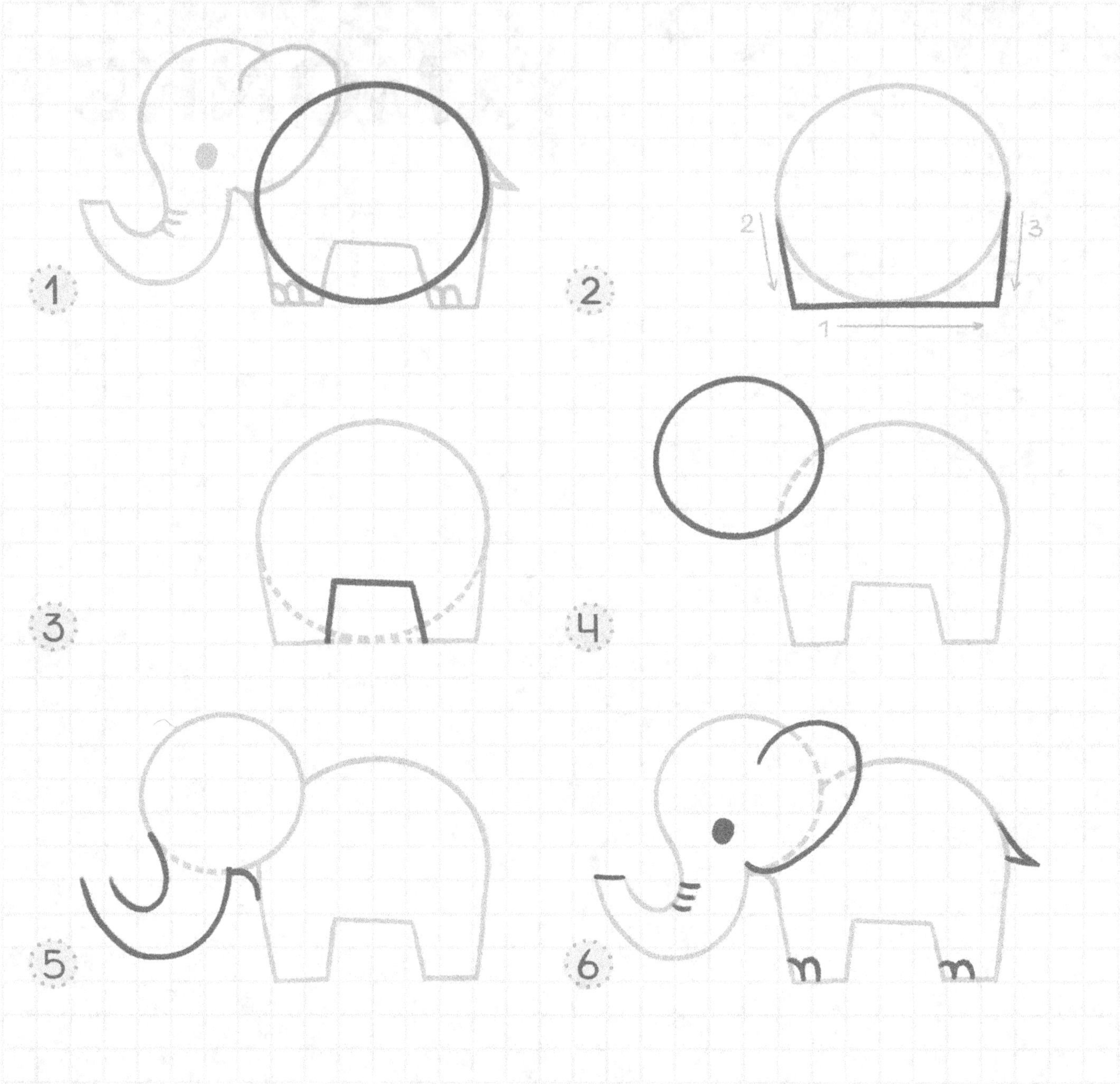

1

2

3

4

5

6

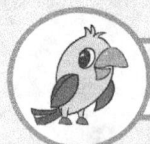 *When elephants get hot, they flap their ears to cool off.*

Elephants are the world's largest land mammals—huge creatures that roam grasslands and rainforests. These smart animals can remember faces, voices, and places with food and water. They use their wiggly trunks to drink, eat, and even spray water like a shower! Elephants roll in red mud to keep bugs away and stay cool. Their tusks are like giant teeth that stick out of their mouths. Tusks help them lift heavy things and dig for water. Baby elephants, called **calves**, are born without tusks.

ELEPHANT

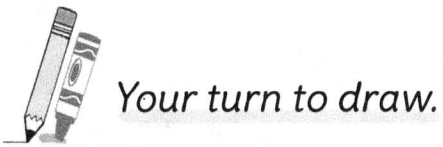 *Your turn to draw.*

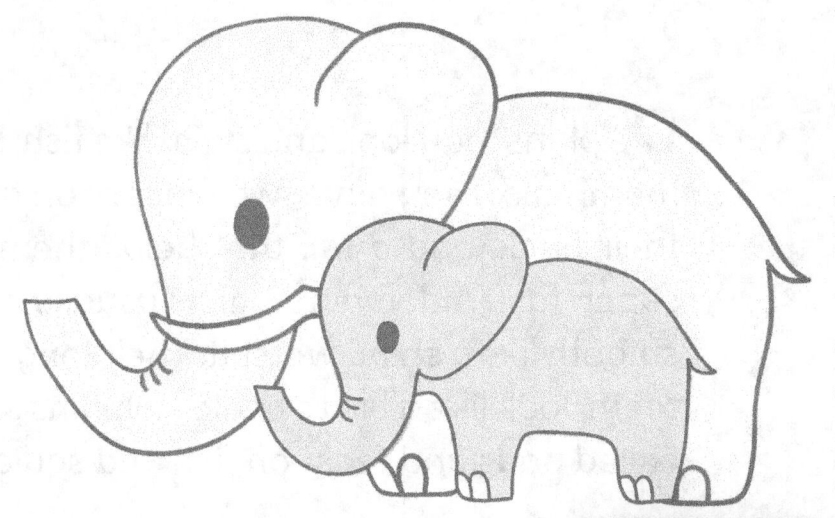

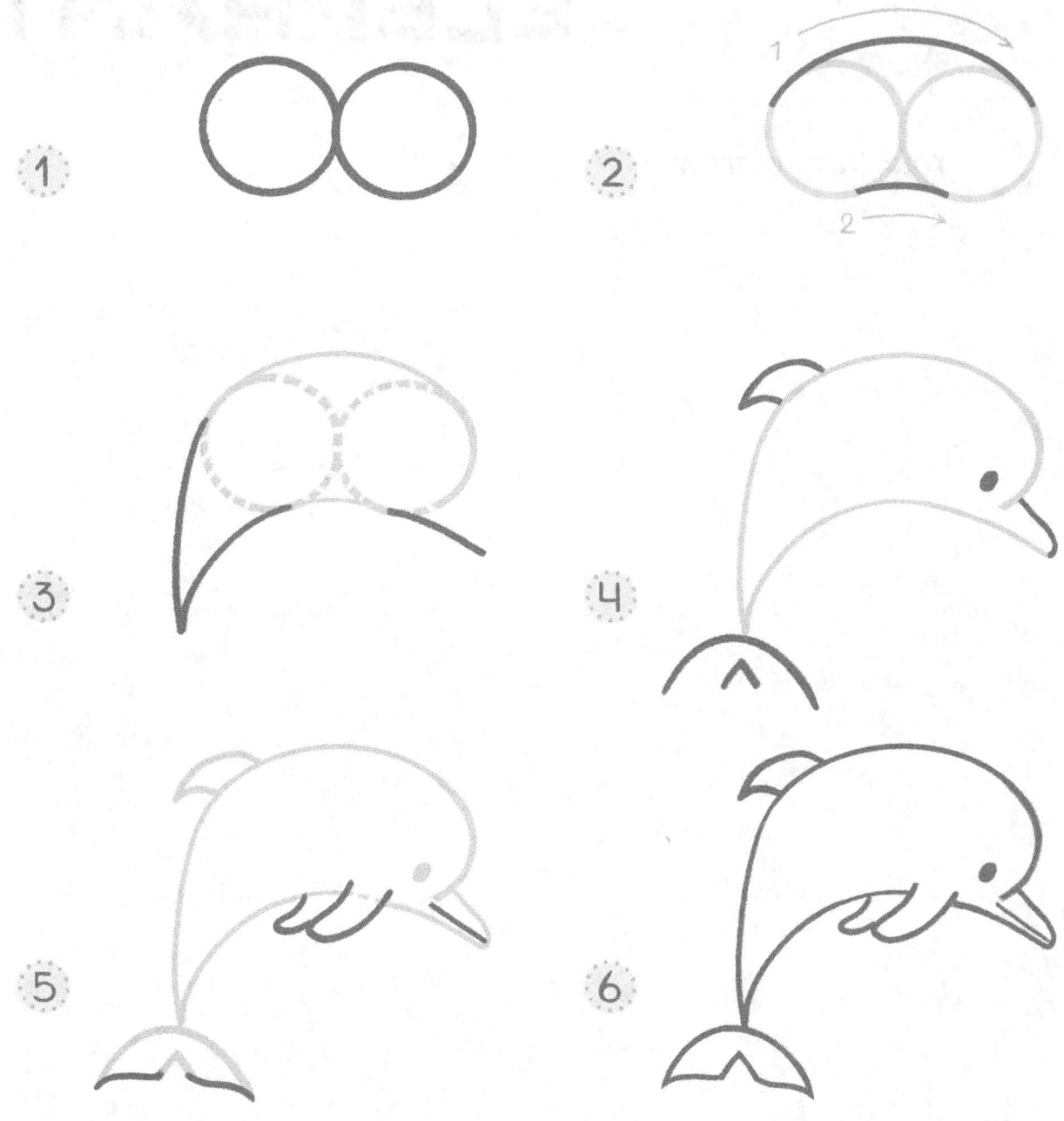

1

2

3

4

5

6

Dolphins may look and swim like fish, but they're actually sea mammals. They have two flippers on their sides, a large fin on their back, and a tail that helps them leap out of the water super-fast. A dolphin's skin is usually a mix of gray and white, smooth like a shiny wetsuit. Their long snouts, filled with sharp teeth, look like a bird's beak. Dolphins swim together in groups called **pods** and feast on fish and squid.

DOLPHIN

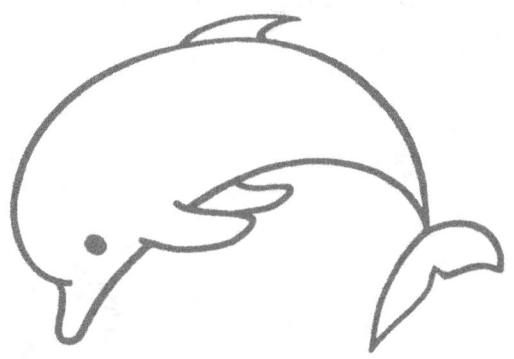

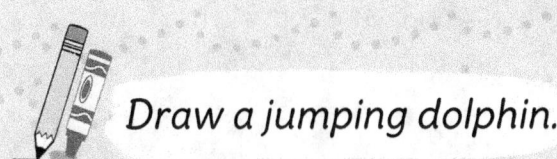

Draw a jumping dolphin.

Birds are amazing—they can be as tiny as bees or as big as people. They're covered in feathers that help them fly and stay warm. Birds have two wings, two legs, a tail, and a beak—also known as a **bill**. They use their beaks for many things, like building nests for their eggs and feeding their babies, called **chicks**. Baby birds need their parents to take care of them until they're ready to leave the nest.

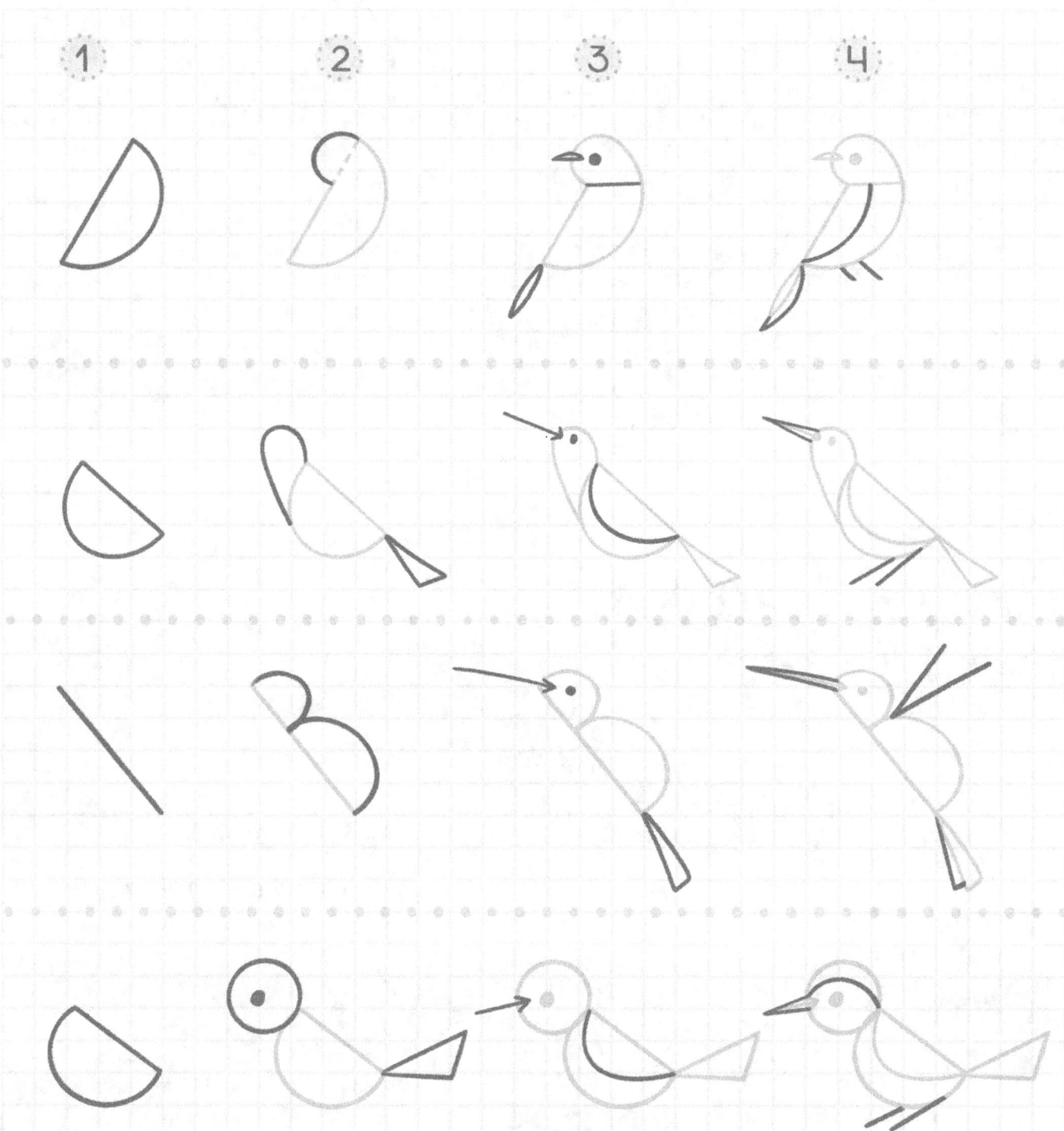

Animals by Alisa Bloom | Draw & Learn™ Book Series

BIRDS

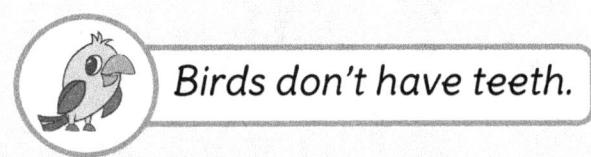 Birds don't have teeth.

5 Your turn to draw birds.

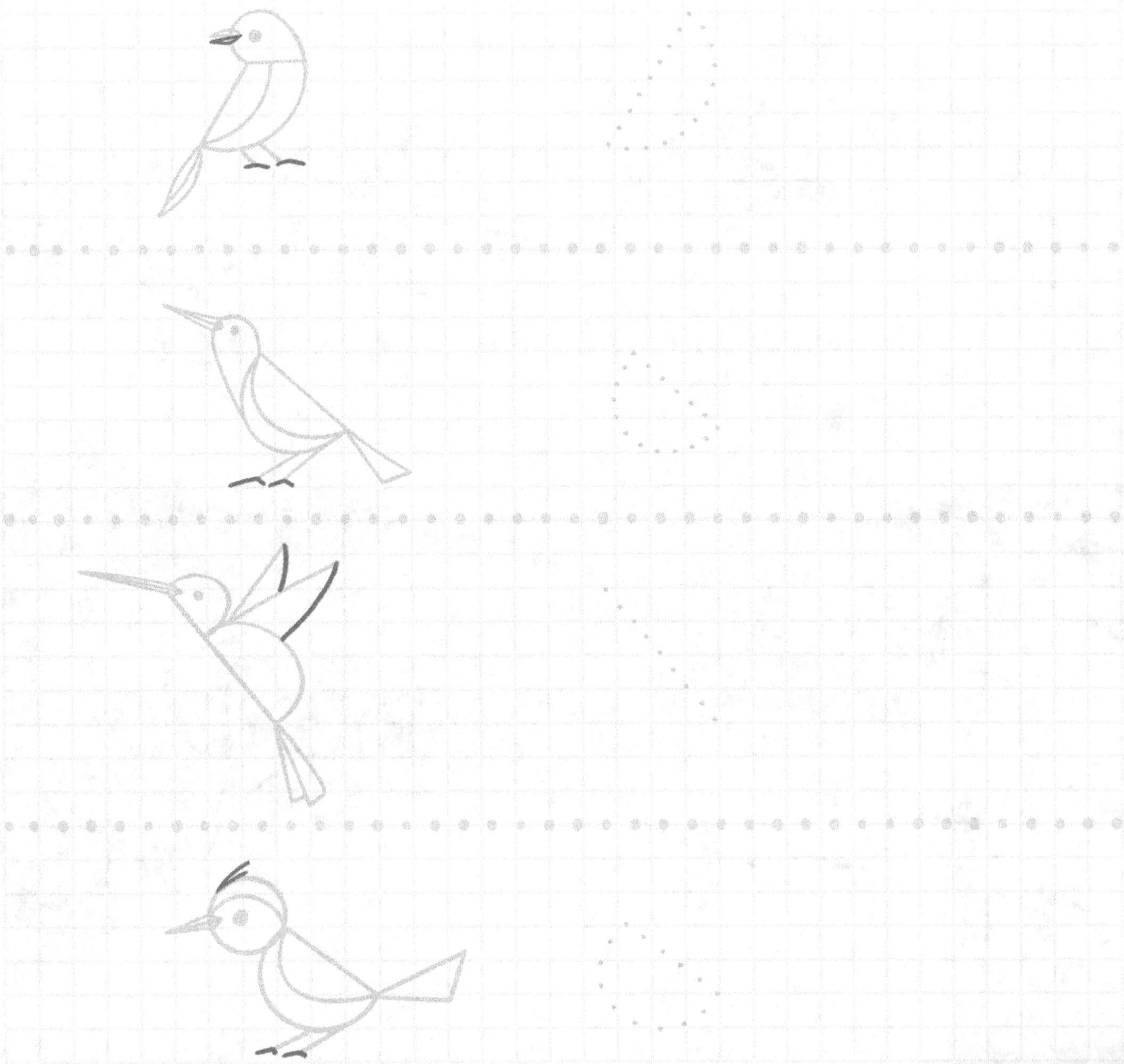

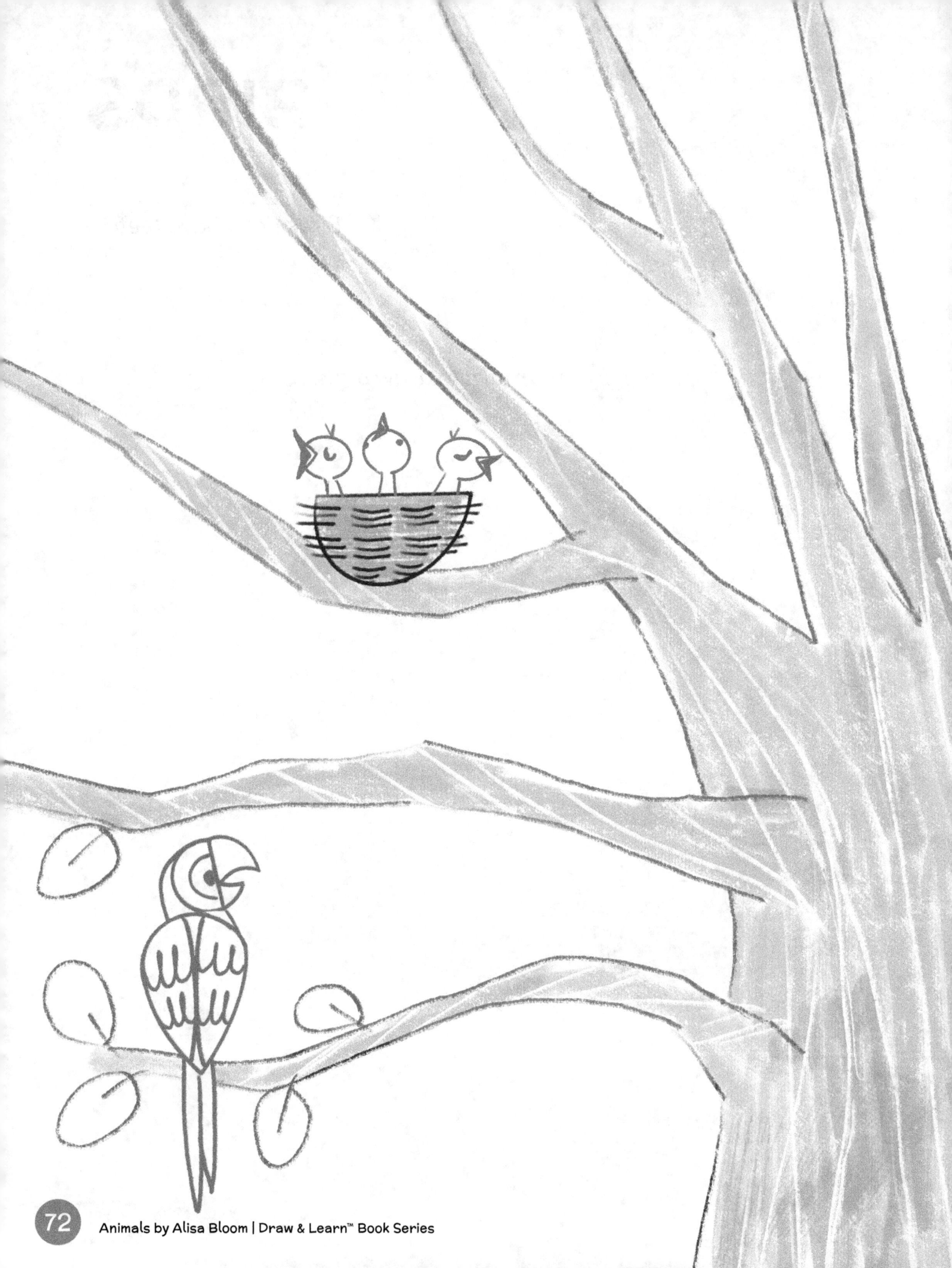

Animals by Alisa Bloom | Draw & Learn™ Book Series

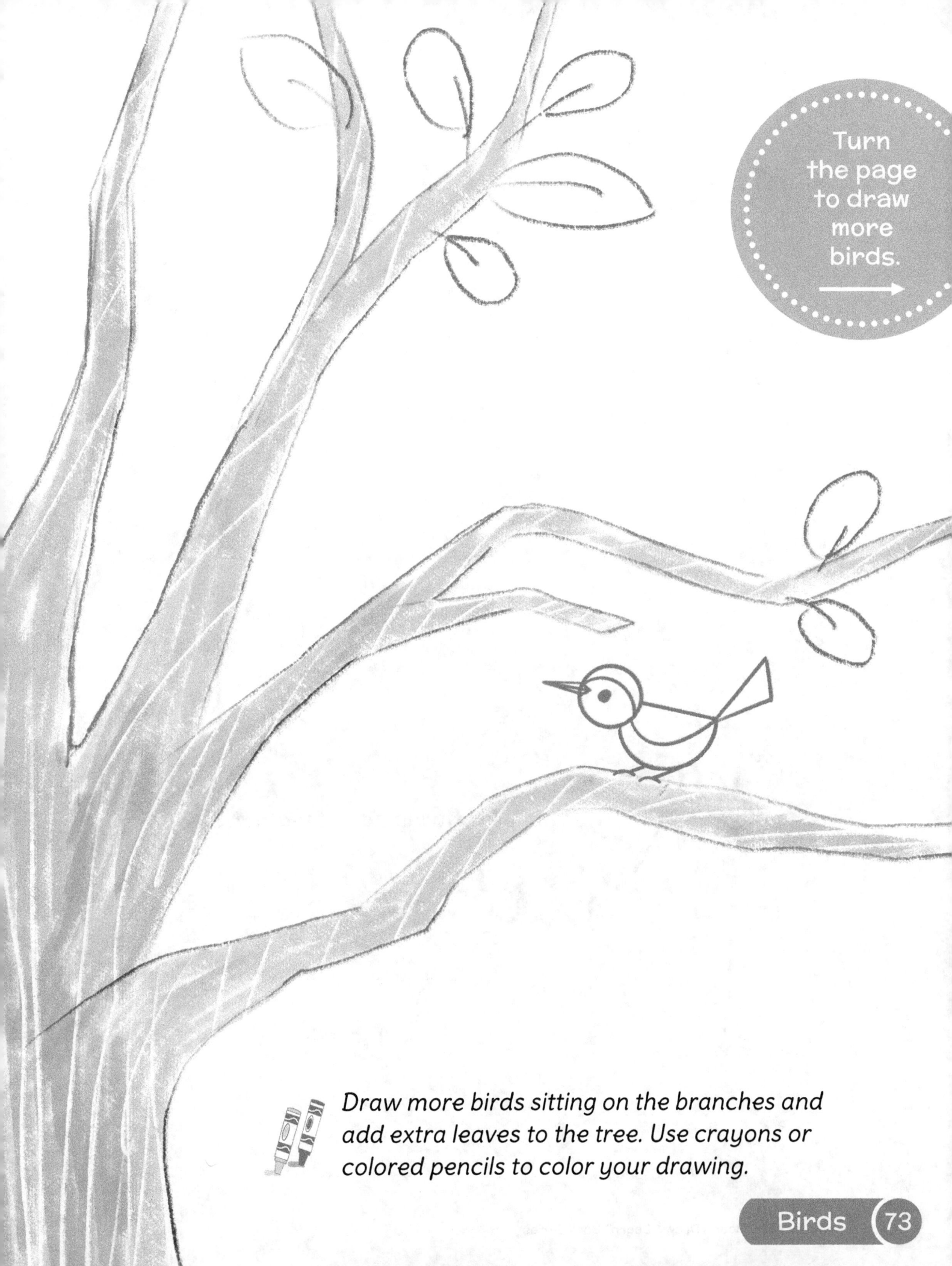

Turn the page to draw more birds. →

Draw more birds sitting on the branches and add extra leaves to the tree. Use crayons or colored pencils to color your drawing.

Birds 73

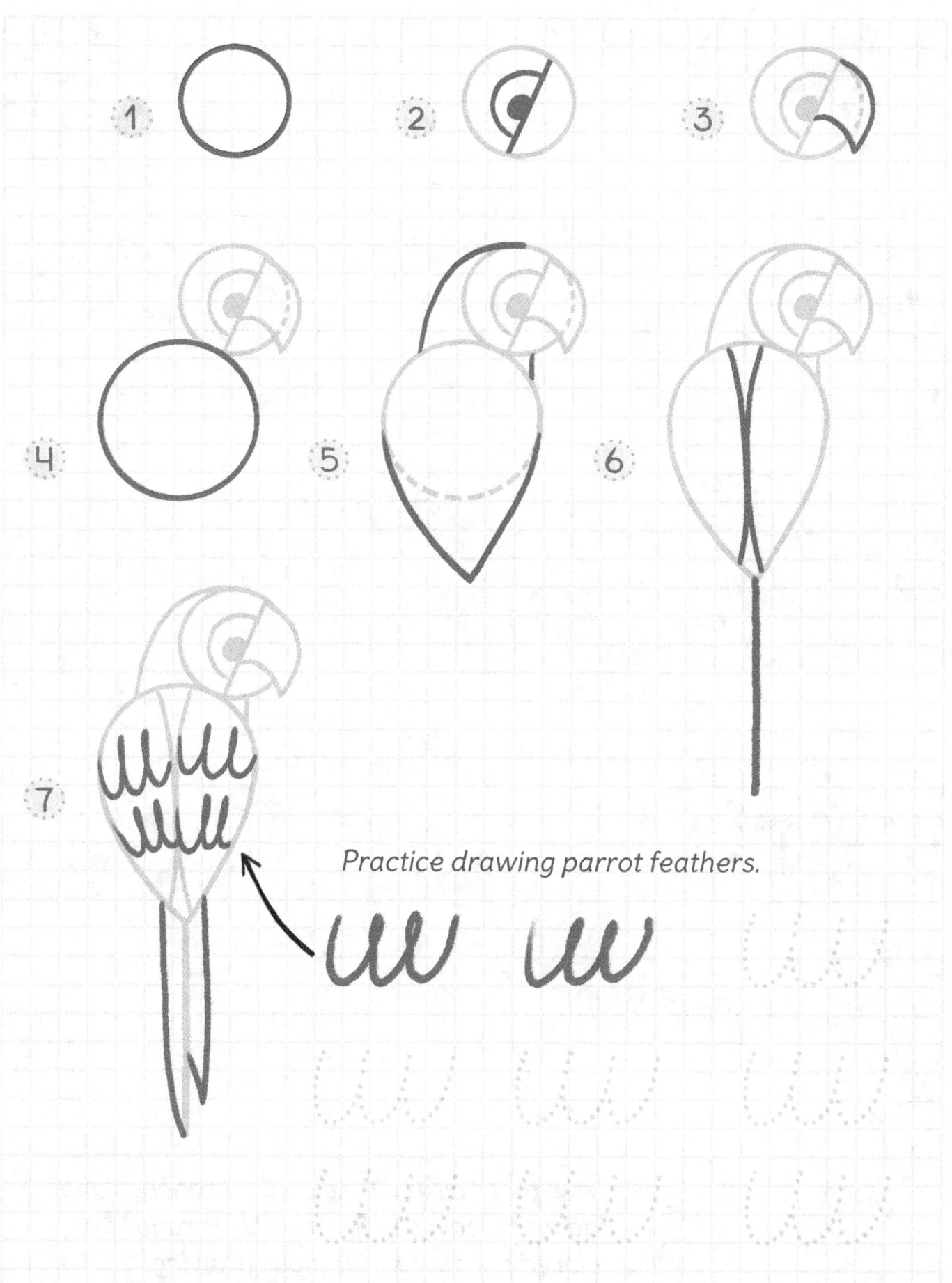

1

2

3

4

5

6

7

Practice drawing parrot feathers.

Animals by Alisa Bloom | Draw & Learn™ Book Series

PARROT

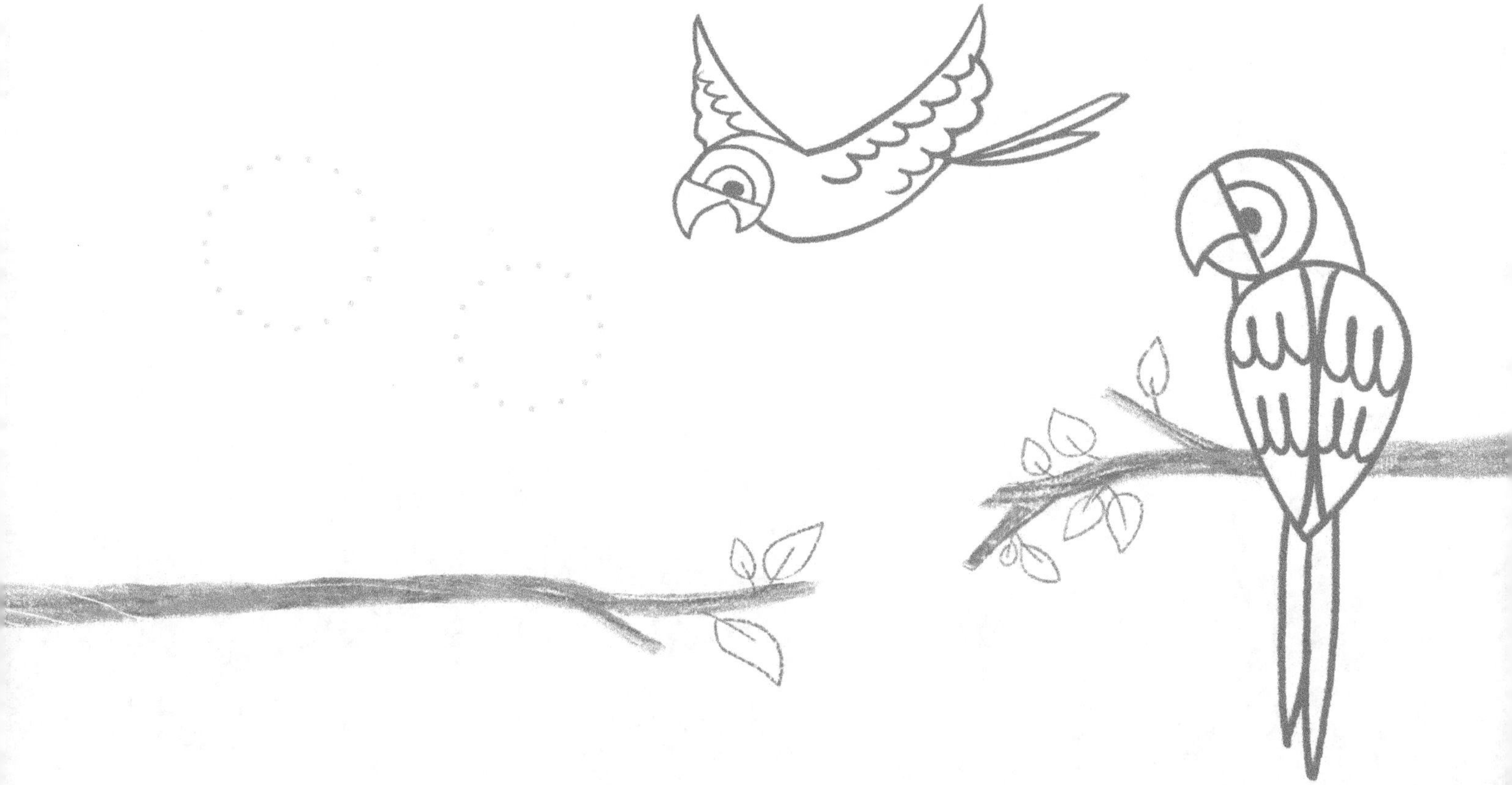

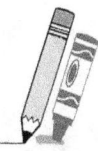 *Draw two parrots sitting on the branch above.*

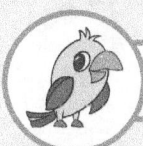 *Parrots can grab and hold food with their toes.*

Parrots are lively birds found in many habitats, from tropical forests to frosty mountains. Their feathers can be bright blue, green, orange, red, yellow, or a mix of these colors. With their strong, hook-shaped beaks, parrots can crack open tough shells and climb trees. They love snacking on seeds, nuts, fruit, vegetables, and sometimes bugs. Many parrots are great at copying sounds—they can learn to say words and even short sentences. Imagine having a talking parrot as a friend!

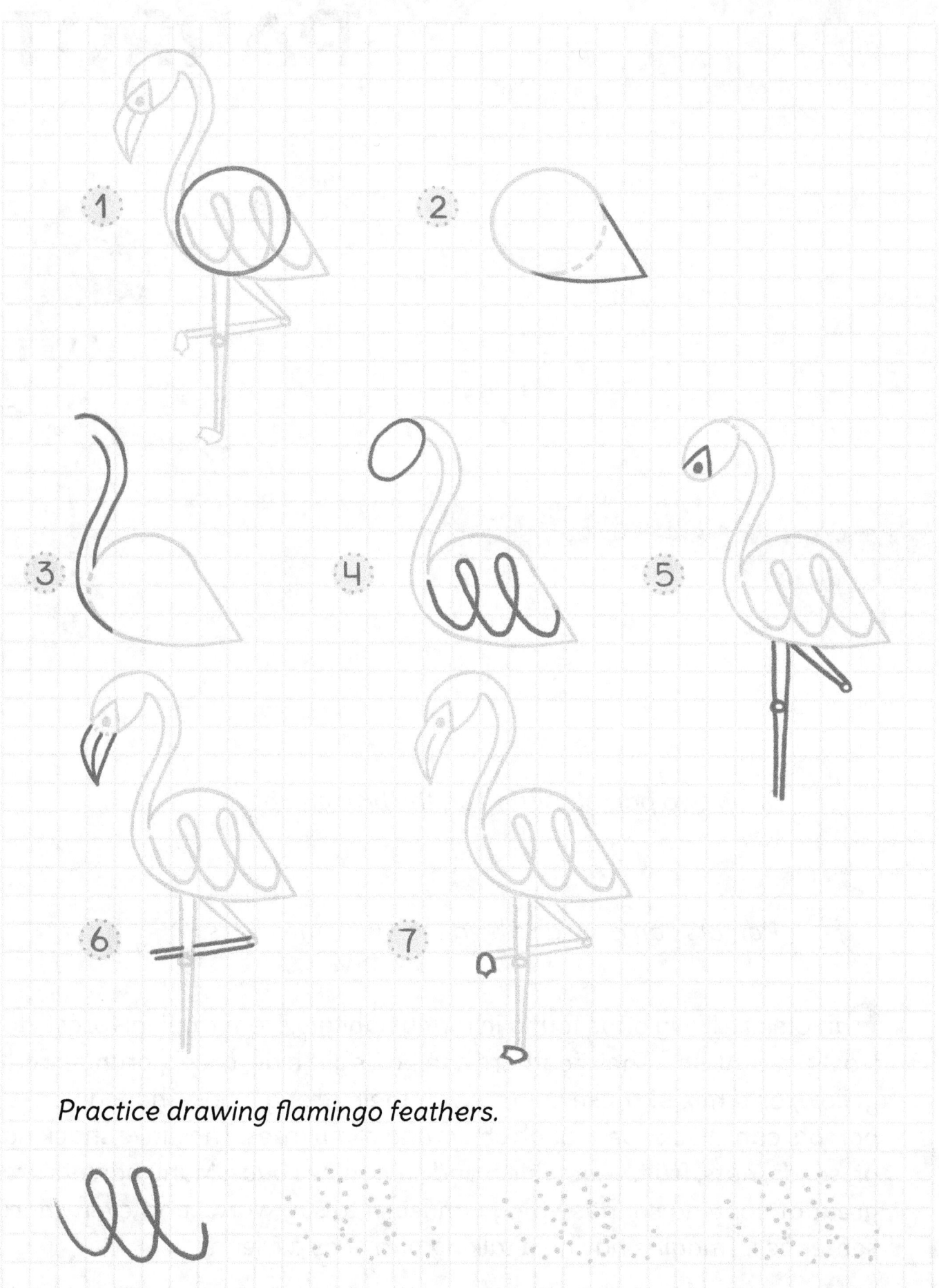

1

2

3

4

5

6

7

Practice drawing flamingo feathers.

FLAMINGO

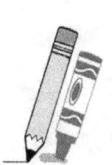 *Draw two flamingos. Start by tracing the shapes above.*

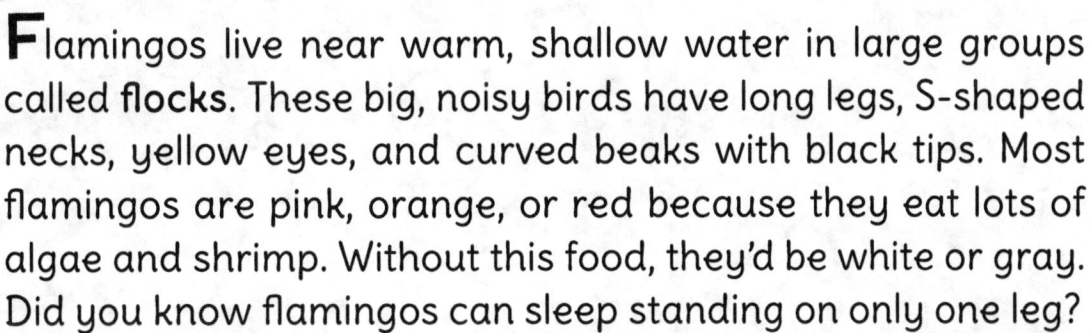

Flamingos live near warm, shallow water in large groups called **flocks**. These big, noisy birds have long legs, S-shaped necks, yellow eyes, and curved beaks with black tips. Most flamingos are pink, orange, or red because they eat lots of algae and shrimp. Without this food, they'd be white or gray. Did you know flamingos can sleep standing on only one leg?

Penguins are birds, but they can't fly. Instead, they use their wings like flippers to swim. Penguins catch and eat fish, krill, and squid. They walk upright and can slide on their bellies over snow and ice. Doesn't that sound like fun? These curious birds sport small round heads, webbed feet, and black backs with white fronts. Most baby penguins have fluffy gray feathers and look incredibly cute.

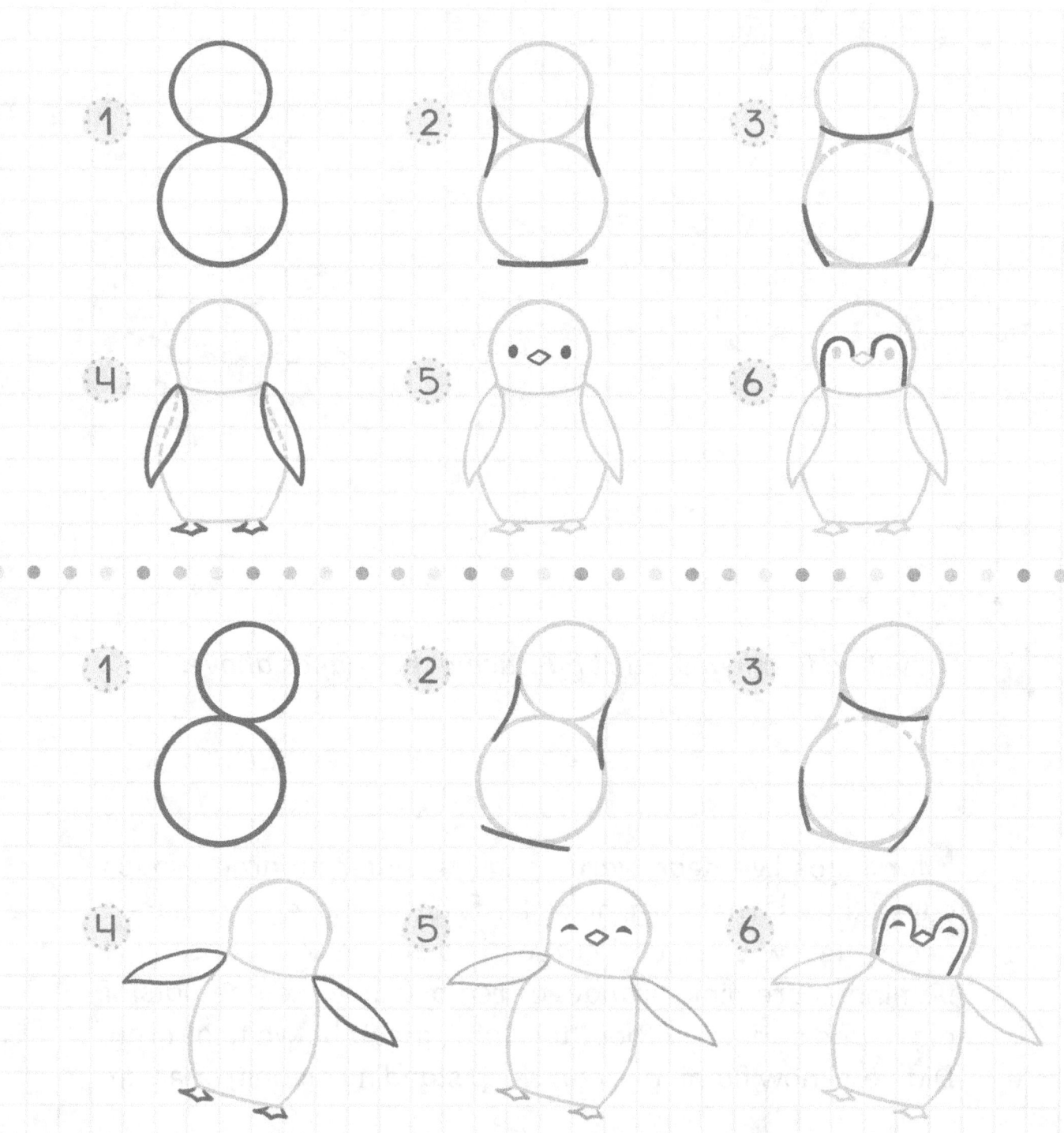

Animals by Alisa Bloom | Draw & Learn™ Book Series

PENGUIN

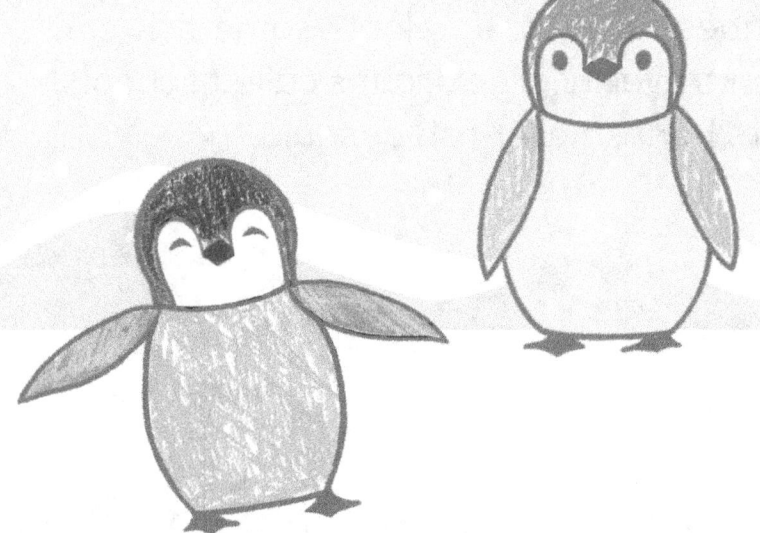

Turn the page to learn about cool fish. →

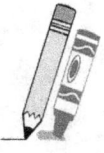 How many penguins can you draw on this page?

Fish live in all kinds of water, including oceans, seas, rivers, lakes, and ponds. They come in many shapes, sizes, and colors—some fish can even glow in the dark! They often travel in large groups called **schools**. While some fish eat plants, others hunt smaller fish or squid.

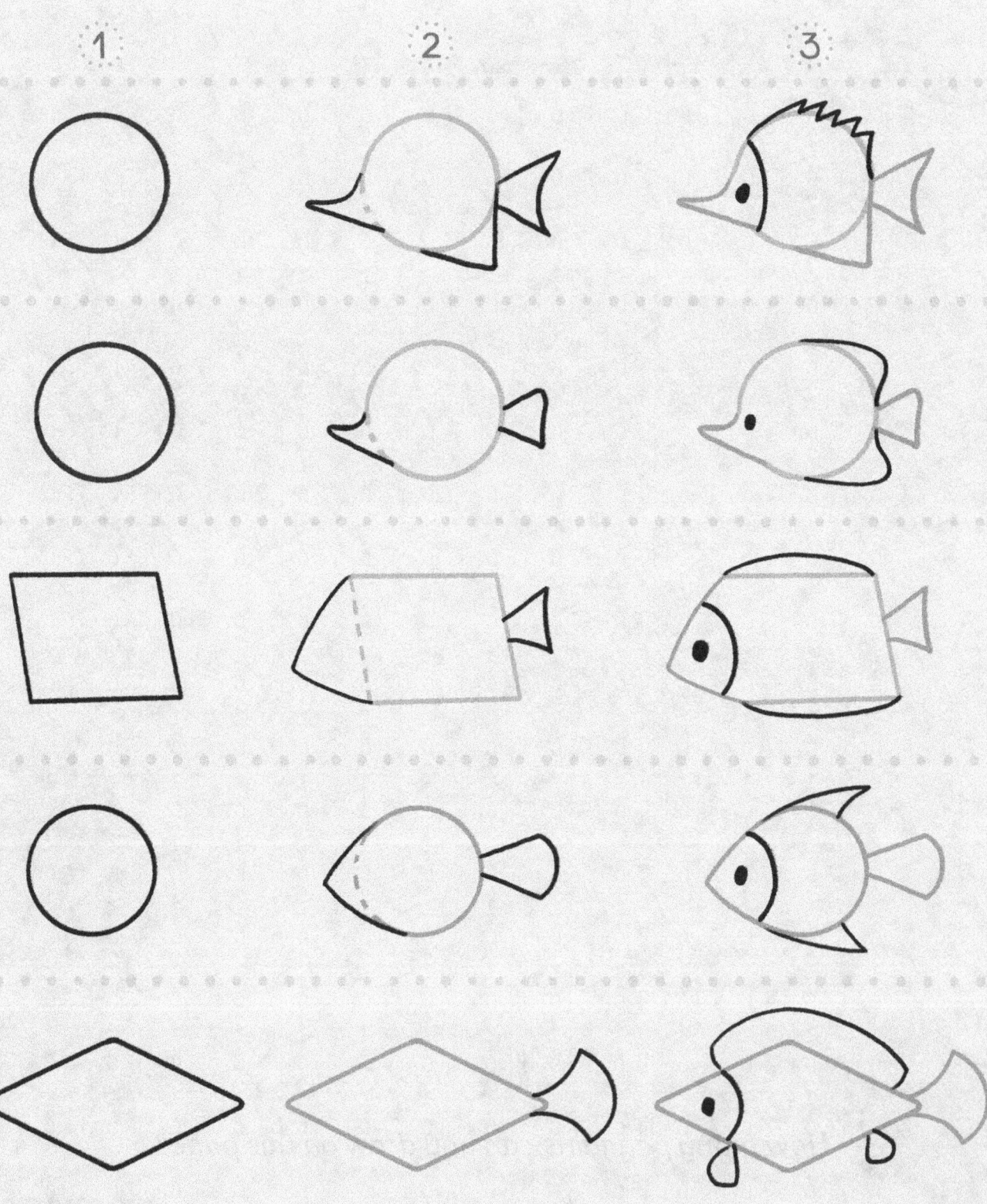

Animals by Alisa Bloom | Draw & Learn™ Book Series

FISH

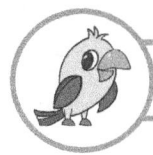 Did you know baby fish are called fry?

4   5   Your turn to draw fish.

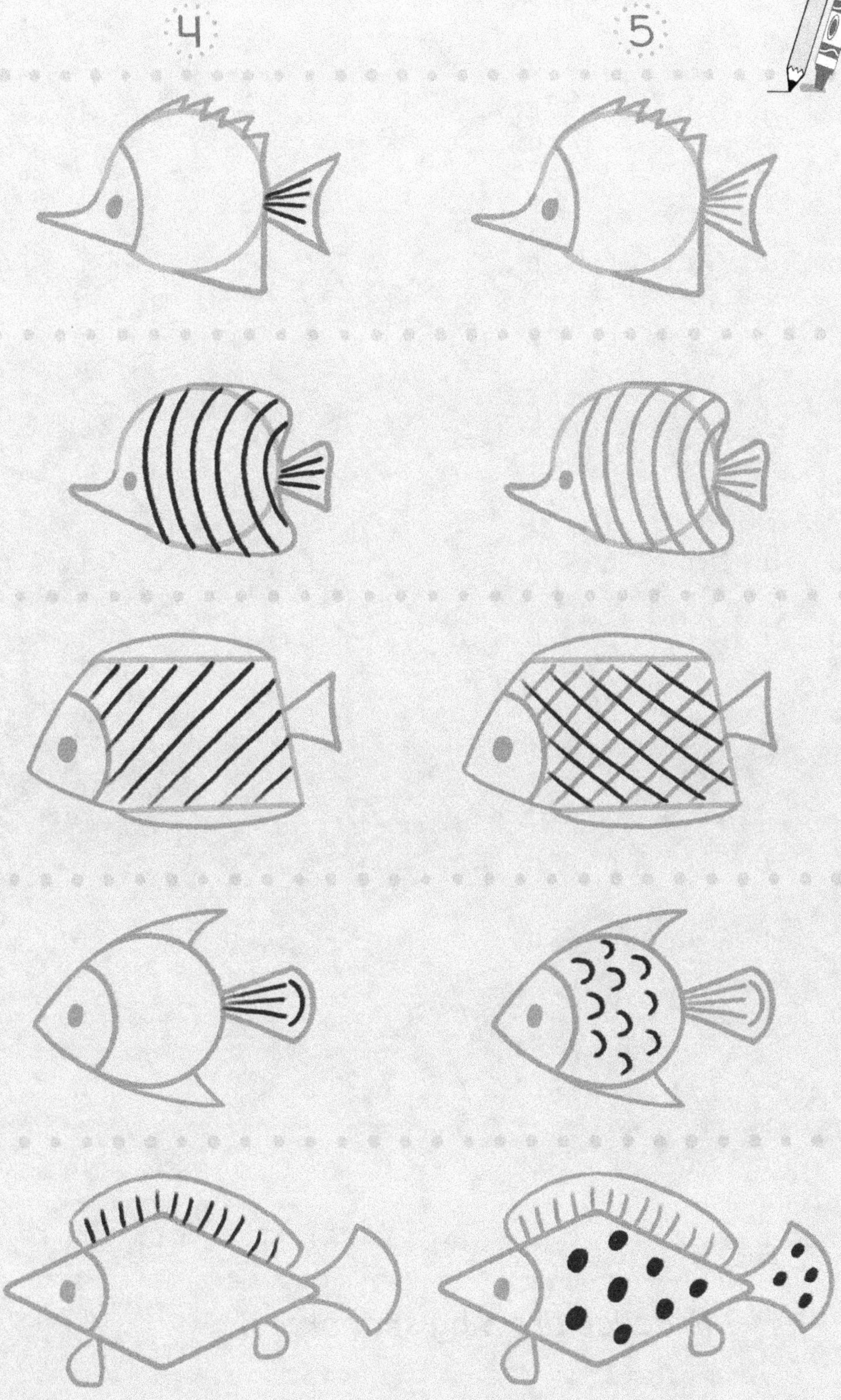

1   2   3   4

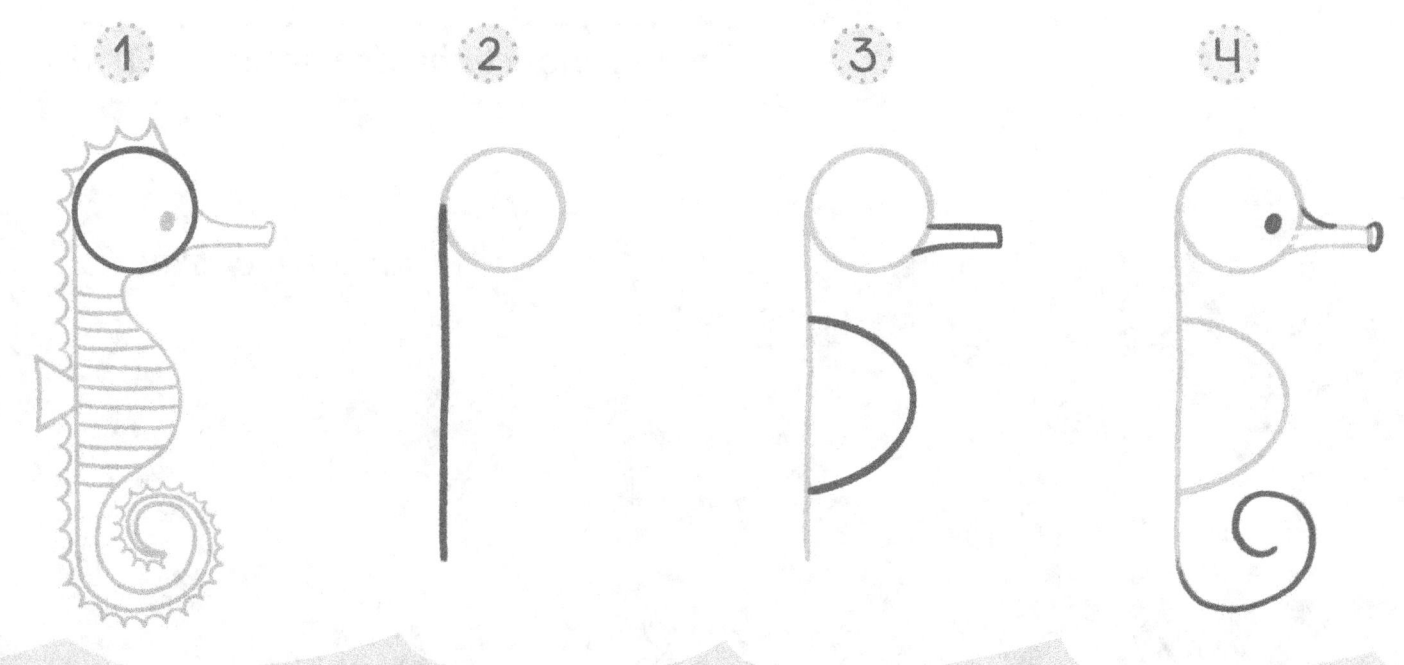

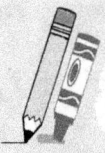 Practice drawing seahorses.

SEAHORSE

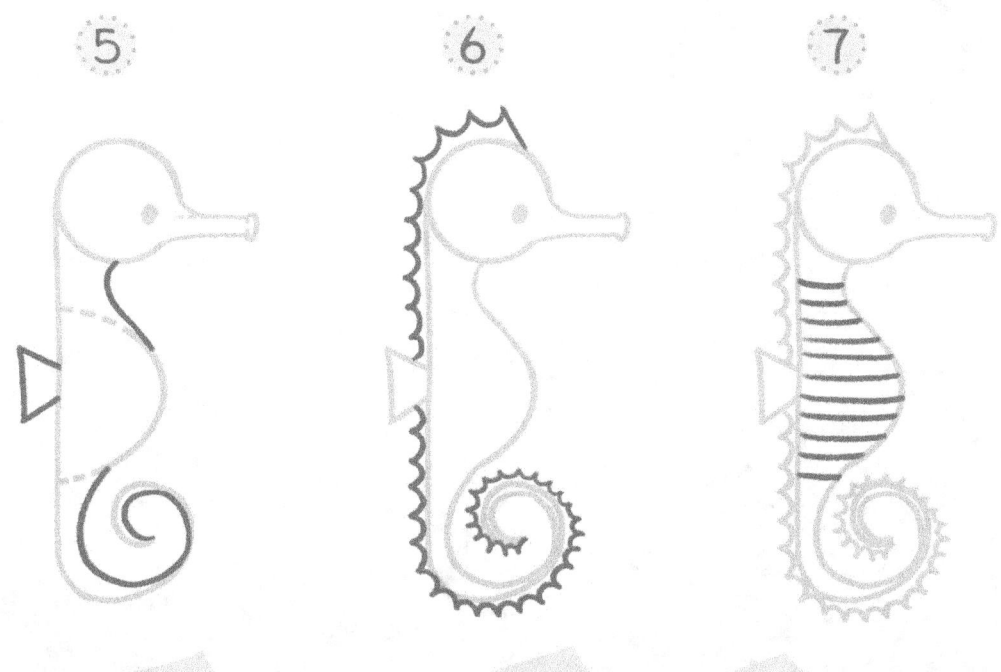

Seahorses are fish. Like other fish, they breathe with gills and swim using fins. Their curly tails help them hang onto sea grass. To sneak up on prey or hide from predators, seahorses can change colors to blend in with plants and corals. Their snouts work like tiny vacuum cleaners, sucking up shrimp, krill, and other small sea creatures.

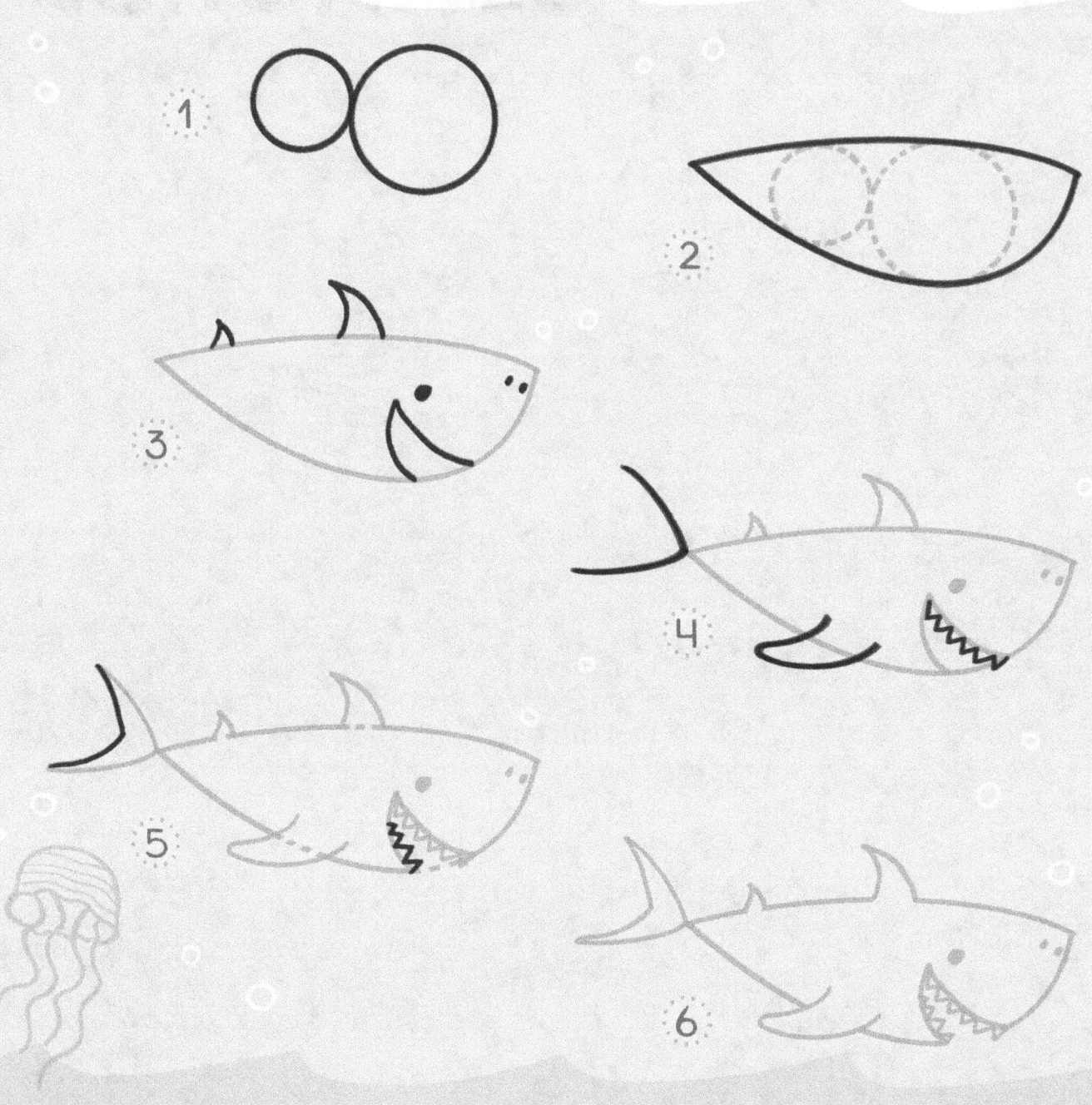

Sharks are fast swimmers and great hunters. They live in the ocean, both near the shore and far out in the deep. Sharks love to chomp on fish, seals, squid, and turtles. Their teeth are super sharp, and new ones grow whenever old ones fall out. Sharks have rough skin that can be blue, brown, gray, or white. Some have stripes or spots. Whale sharks are the biggest fish in the ocean—they can grow as big as a school bus!

SHARK

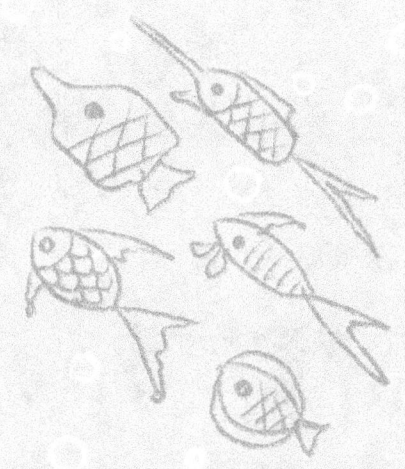

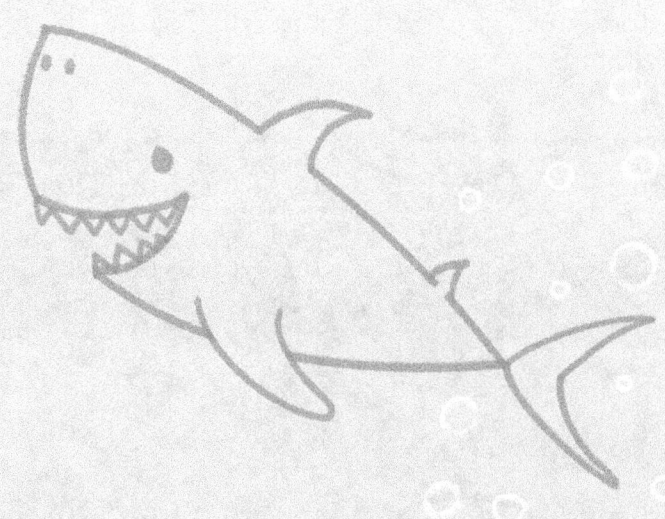

Turn the page to find more fun creatures.
→

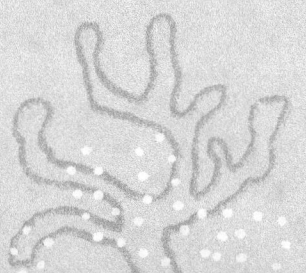 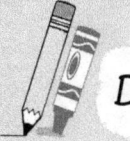 Draw a shark.

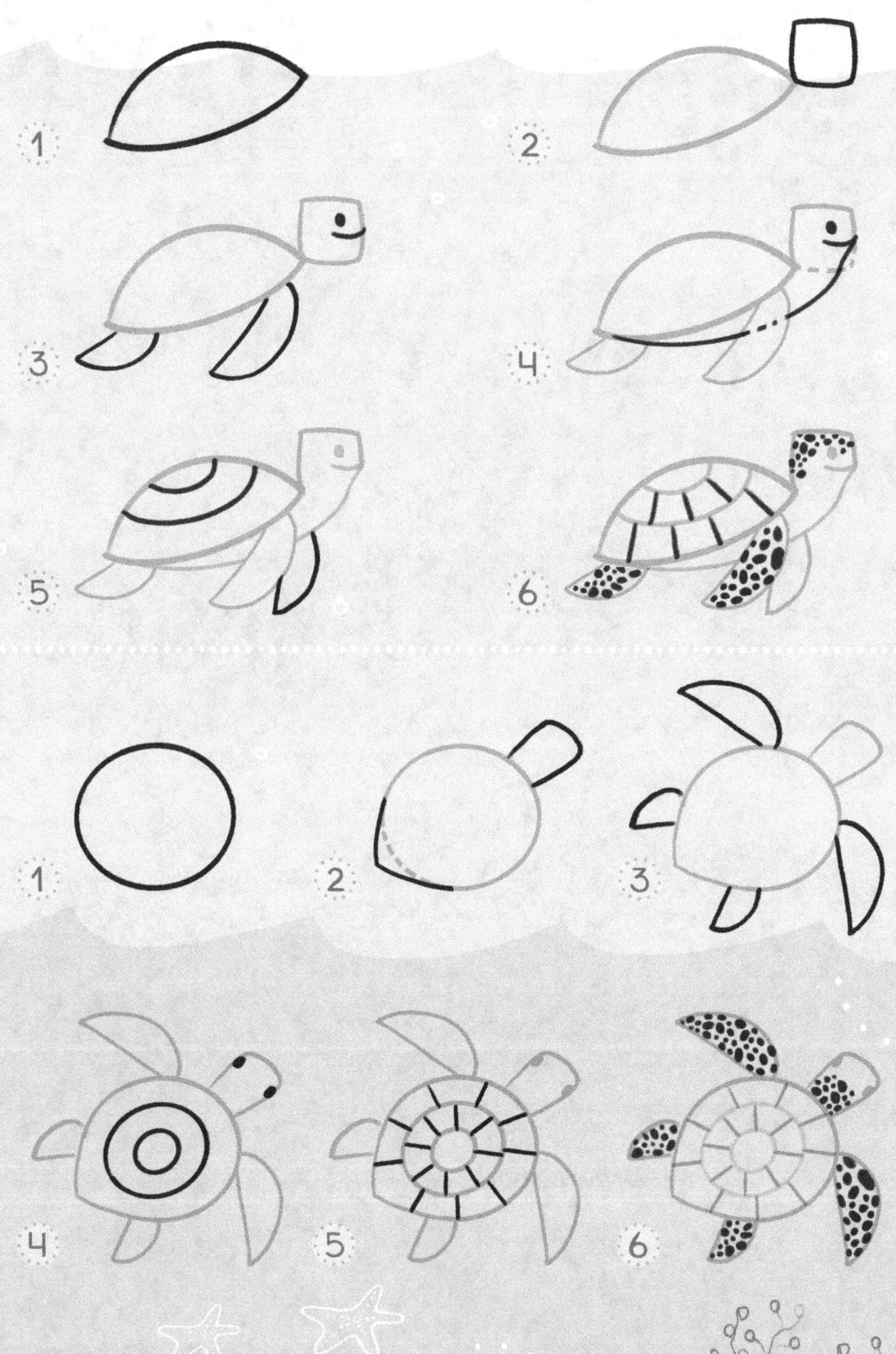

 Animals by Alisa Bloom | Draw & Learn™ Book Series

SEA TURTLE

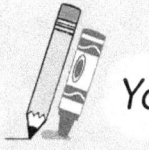 Your turn to draw sea turtles.

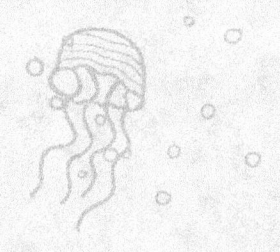

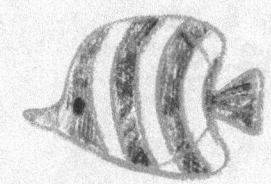

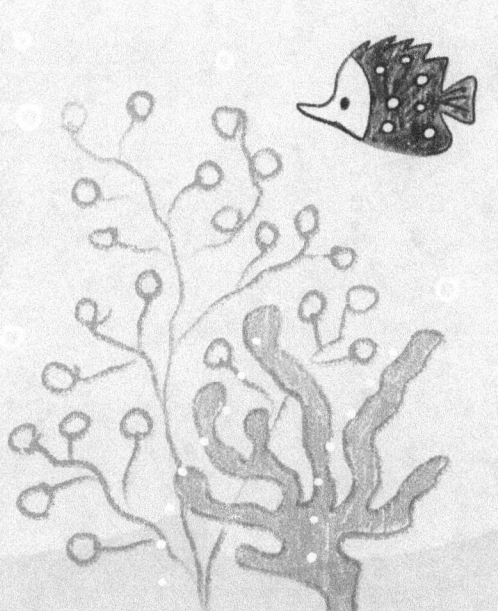

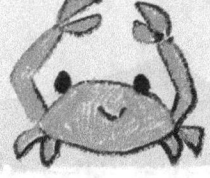

Sea turtles can live for a very long time—over 100 years! They spend most of their lives in the ocean but come to land to lay eggs. These wonderful reptiles breathe air with lungs, just like we do. They use their flippers to swim and dive for algae, seagrass, and other food. Their tough shells, covered with hard plates, keep them safe from predators like sharks. The shells can be black, brown, green, or yellow.

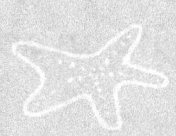

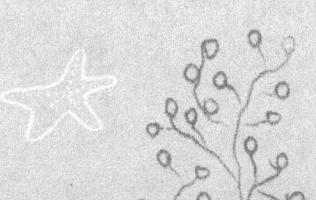

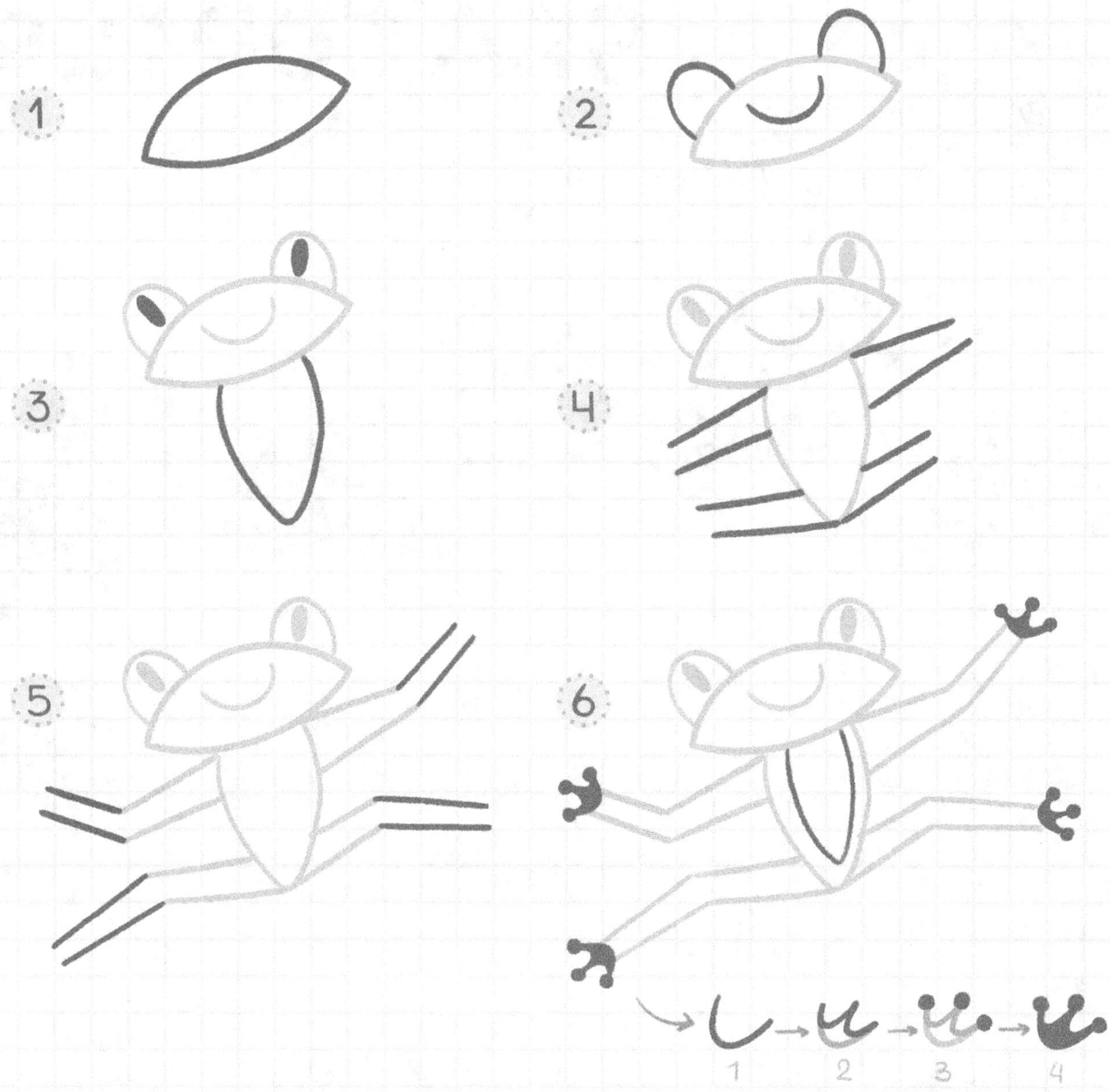

1

2

3

4

5

6

1 2 3 4

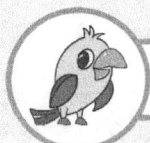 *When baby frogs hatch from eggs, they look like fish.*

Frogs are amphibians that were around even before dinosaurs walked our planet. Baby frogs, called **tadpoles**, live in the water until they grow legs and are ready to hop onto land. These amazing animals can breathe and take in water through their skin. They're incredible jumpers and skilled hunters that eat all kinds of bugs. Most frogs are green, brown, or gray, but watch out for those with very bright colors—they might be poisonous! Can you guess what a group of frogs is called? It's an **army**!

FROG

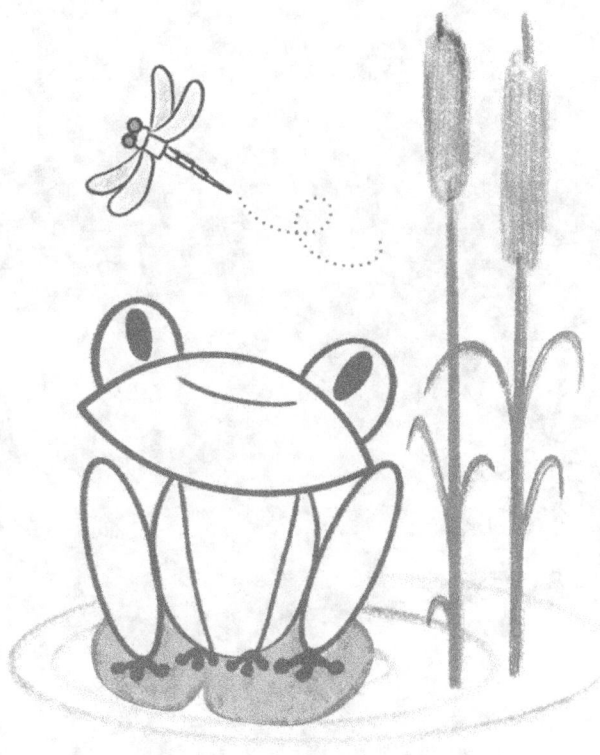

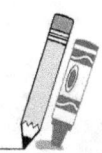 *Draw two jumping frogs and one sitting frog.*

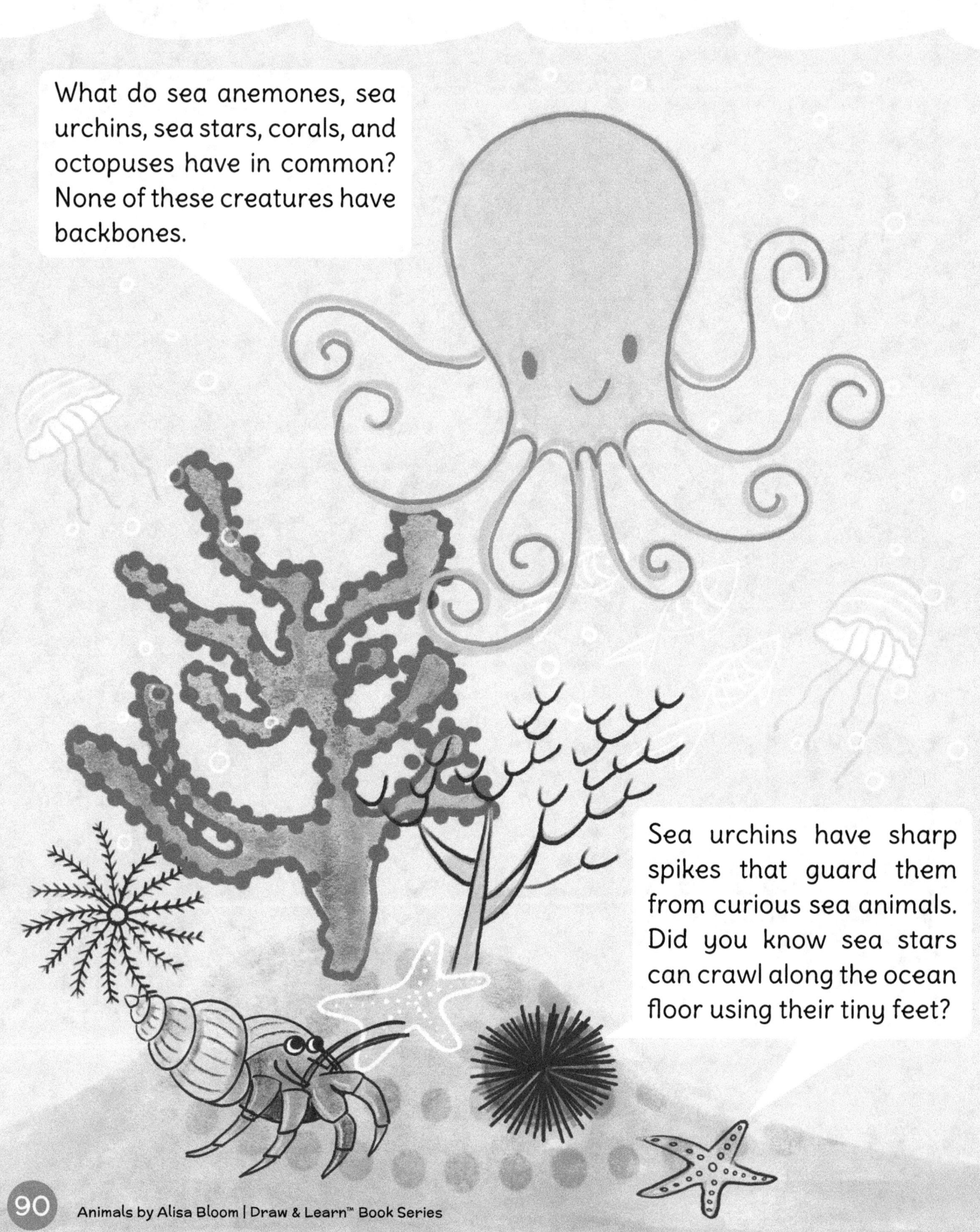

What do sea anemones, sea urchins, sea stars, corals, and octopuses have in common? None of these creatures have backbones.

Sea urchins have sharp spikes that guard them from curious sea animals. Did you know sea stars can crawl along the ocean floor using their tiny feet?

Animals by Alisa Bloom | Draw & Learn™ Book Series

UNDER the SEA

Corals are large colonies of tiny sea animals known as polyps. They can look like colorful flowers or tree branches.

Sea anemones come in many shapes, such as tubes and flowers.

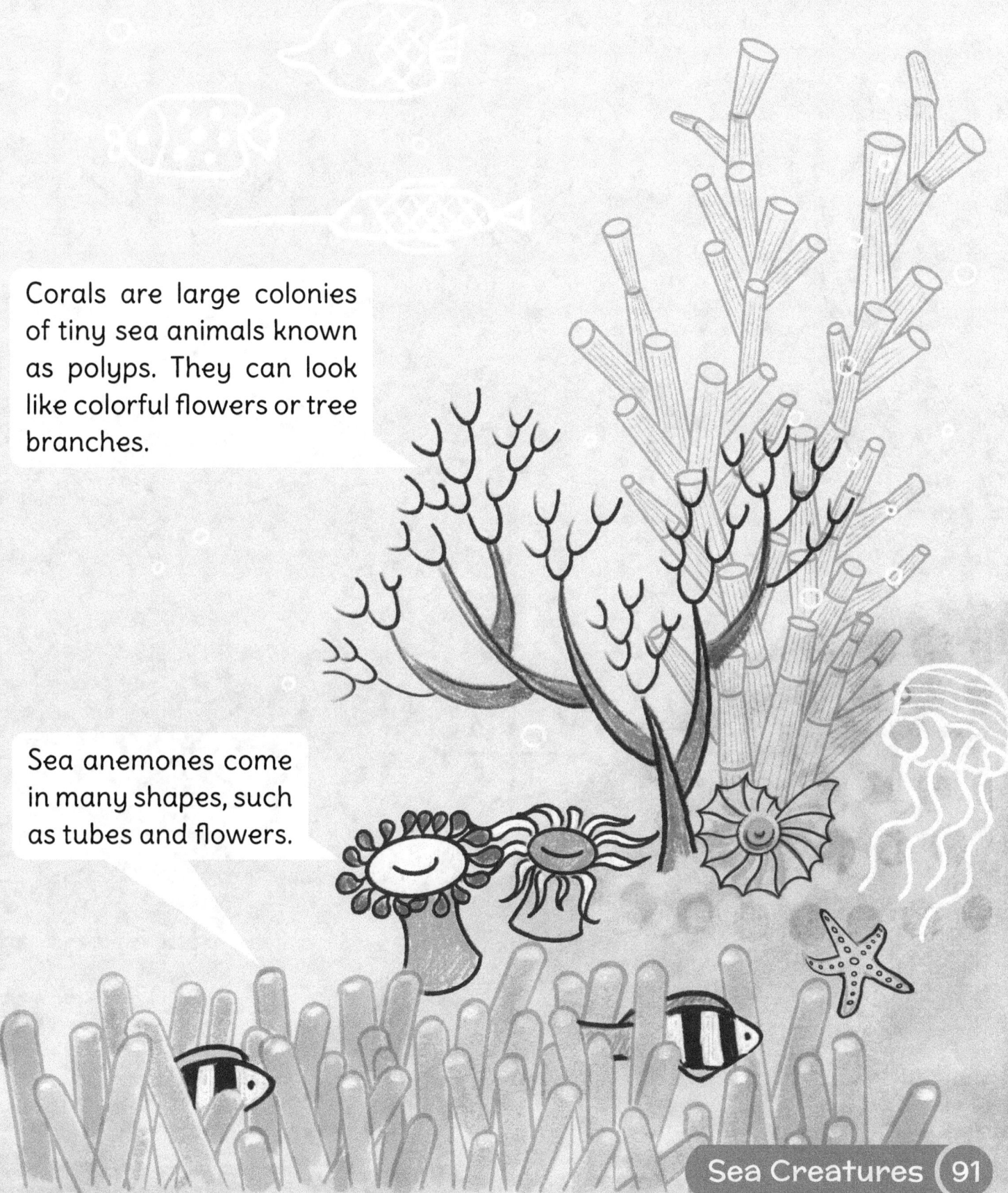

Sea anemones, sea stars, sea urchins, and corals all live near the ocean floor. They come in many bright colors and are fun to look at.

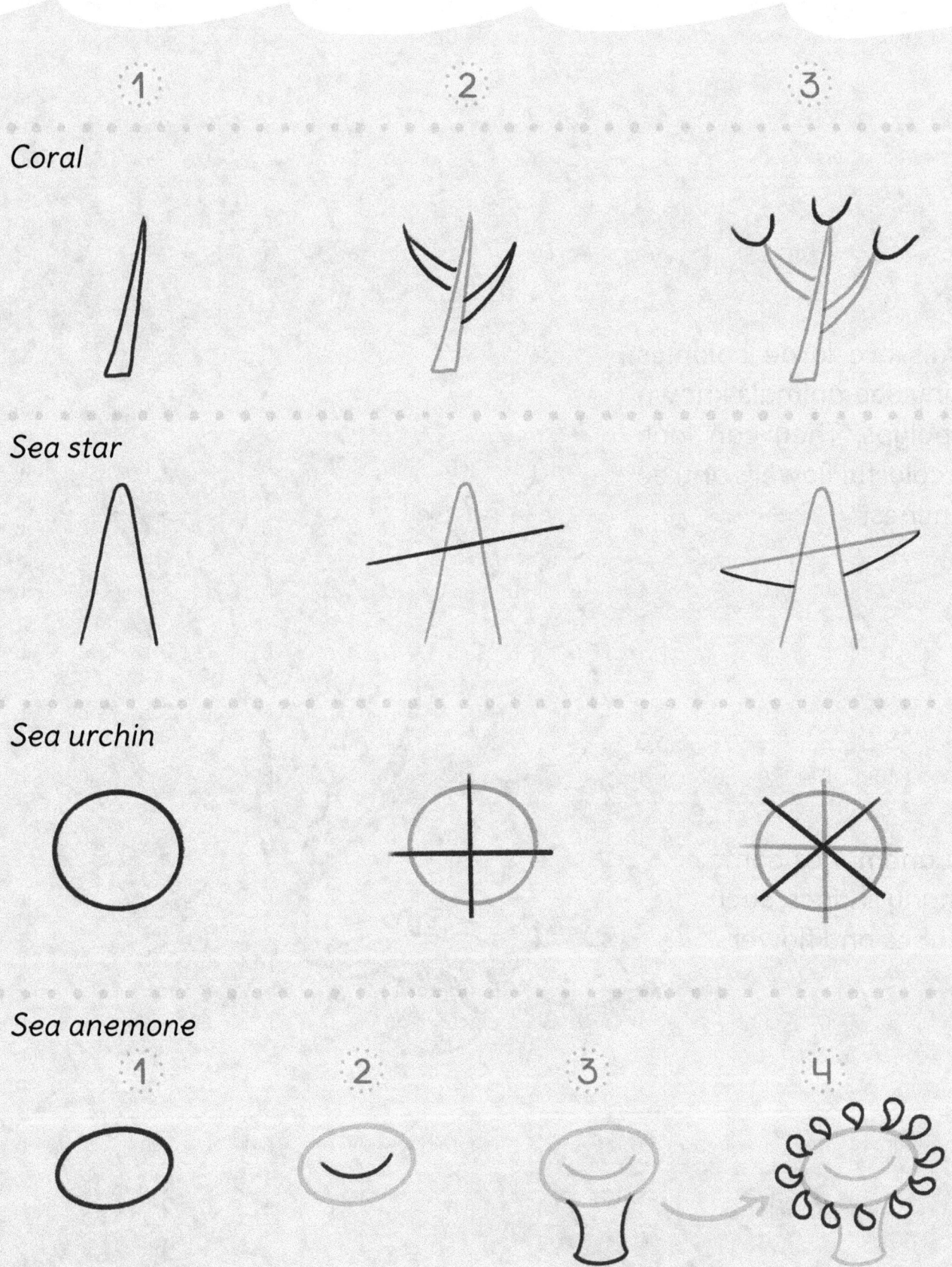

Coral

Sea star

Sea urchin

Sea anemone

Animals by Alisa Bloom | Draw & Learn™ Book Series

BONELESS SEA CREATURES

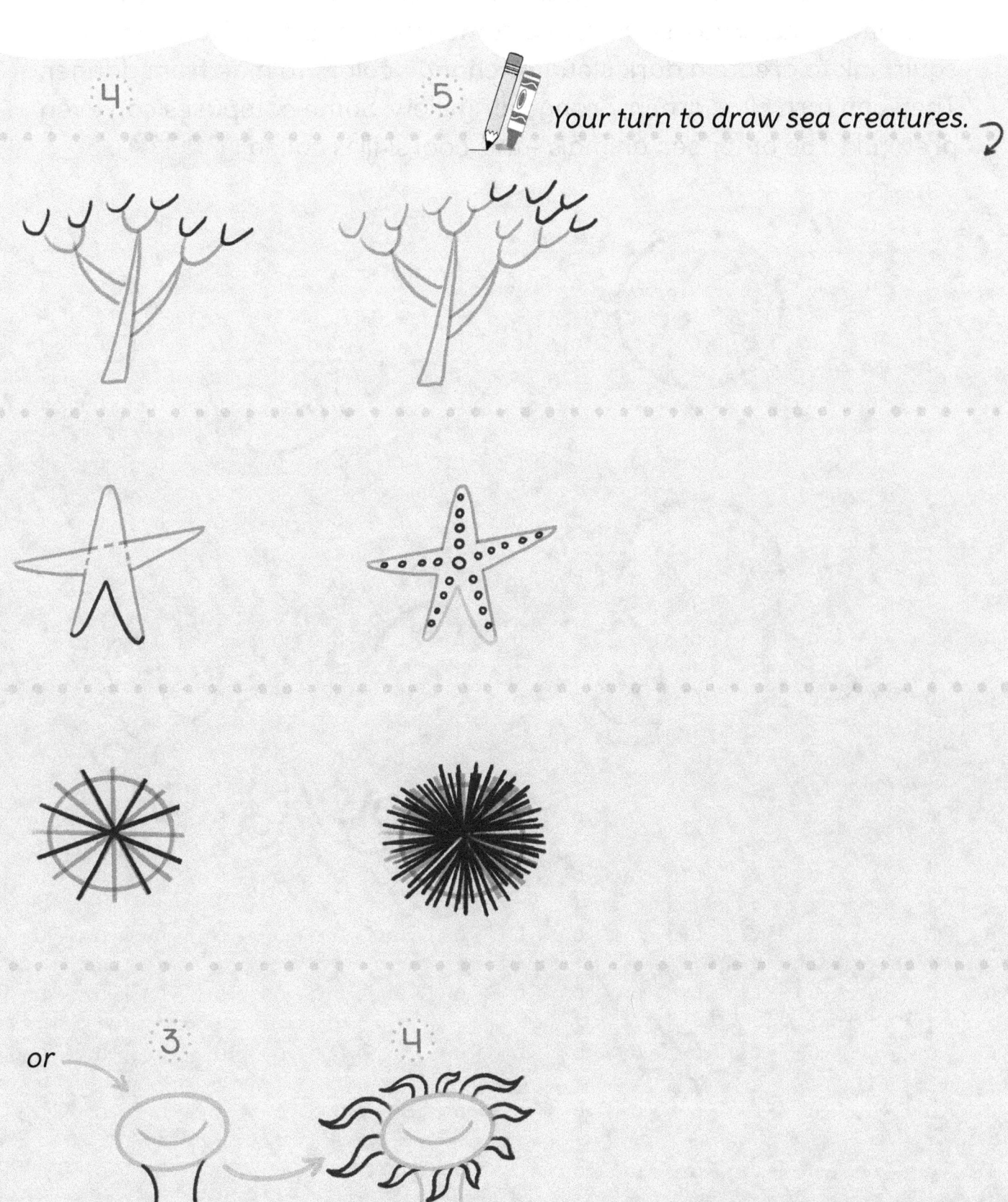

4

5

Your turn to draw sea creatures.

or

3

4

Octopuses are mollusks, just like squids and snails. They have large heads, big eyes, and eight long arms covered with sticky suckers. Baby octopuses hatch from soft eggs that look like grains of rice. As they grow, they eat clams, crabs, shrimp, and sometimes small fish. Octopuses can squirt ink to create a dark cloud or change colors to hide from danger. They can turn blue, green, orange, or yellow. Some octopuses can even pretend to be other sea animals—this cool skill is called mimicry.

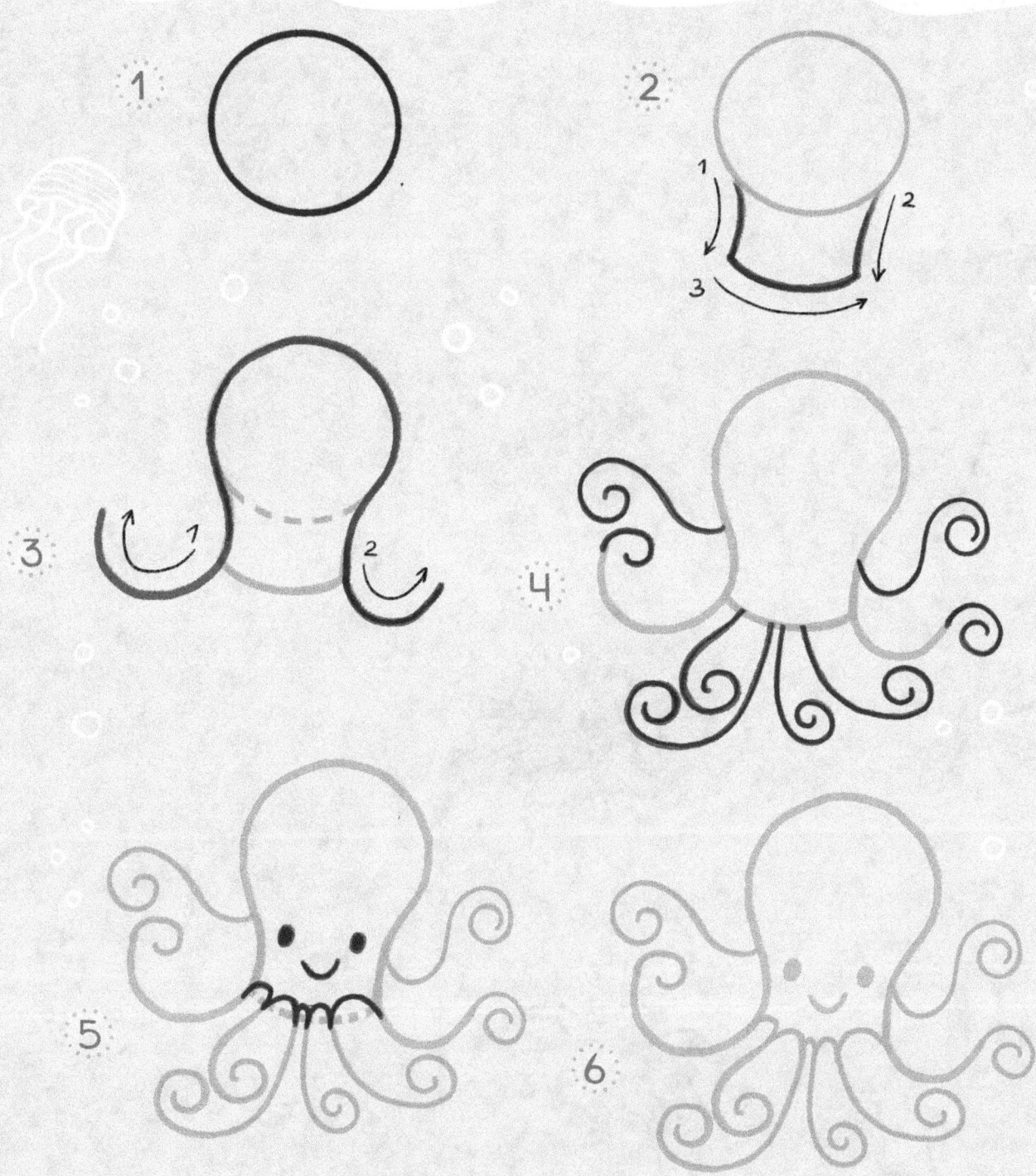

Animals by Alisa Bloom | Draw & Learn™ Book Series

OCTOPUS

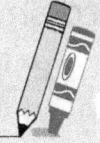

Turn the circle above into an octopus.

SNAIL

Beetles, butterflies, snails, and spiders may look different, but they all share one special trait: they don't have backbones.

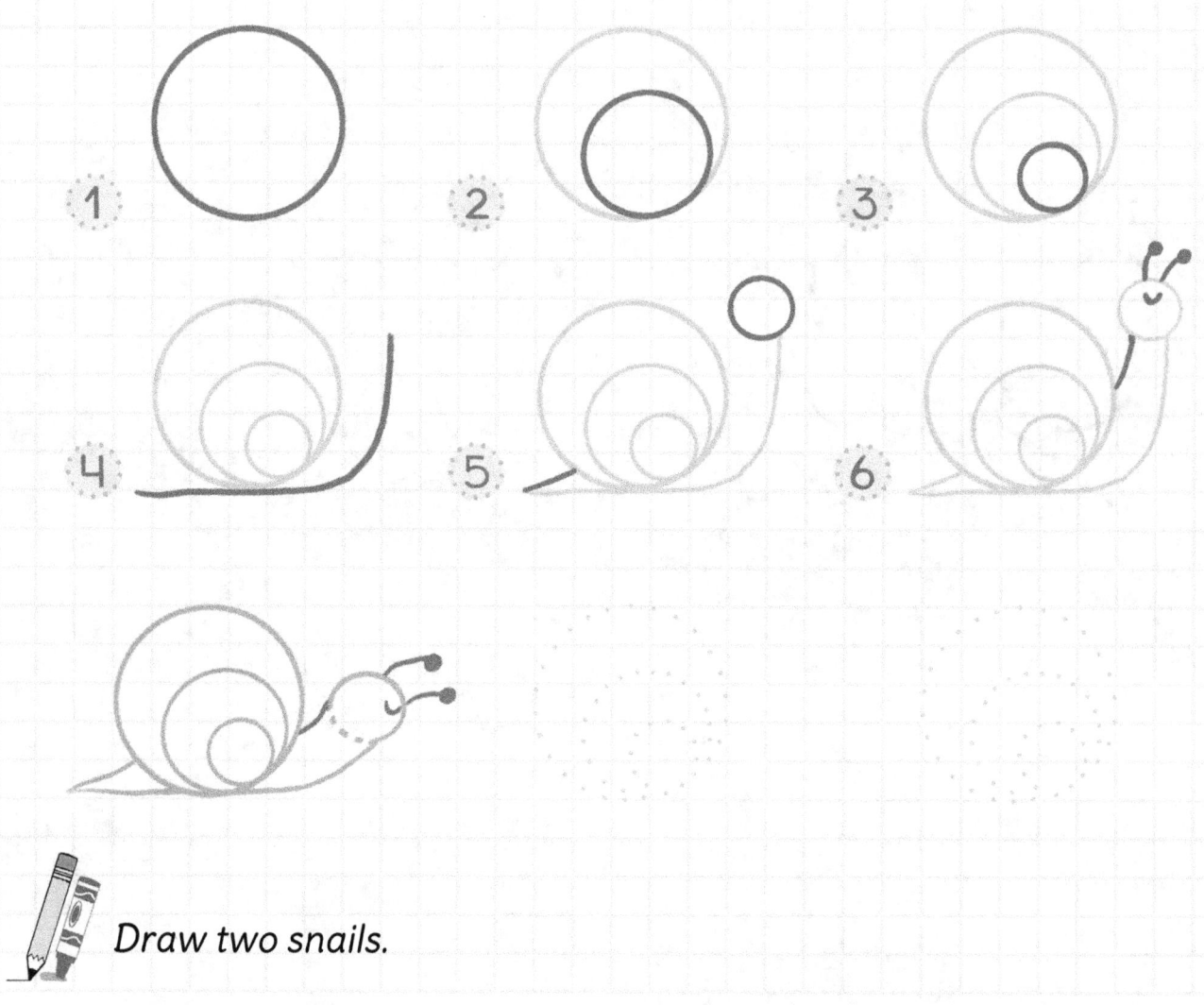

Draw two snails.

Snails live in lots of places, including grasslands, forests, deserts, and oceans. They have soft bodies with hard shells and no legs. They slide on their bellies, moving only a few feet per minute. That's even slower than a turtle! Their shells protect them from predators and the sun's heat. As snails grow, their shells grow and twist along with them. With eyes at the tips of their long tentacles, these curious animals are always ready to explore their surroundings.

Animals by Alisa Bloom | Draw & Learn™ Book Series

SPIDER

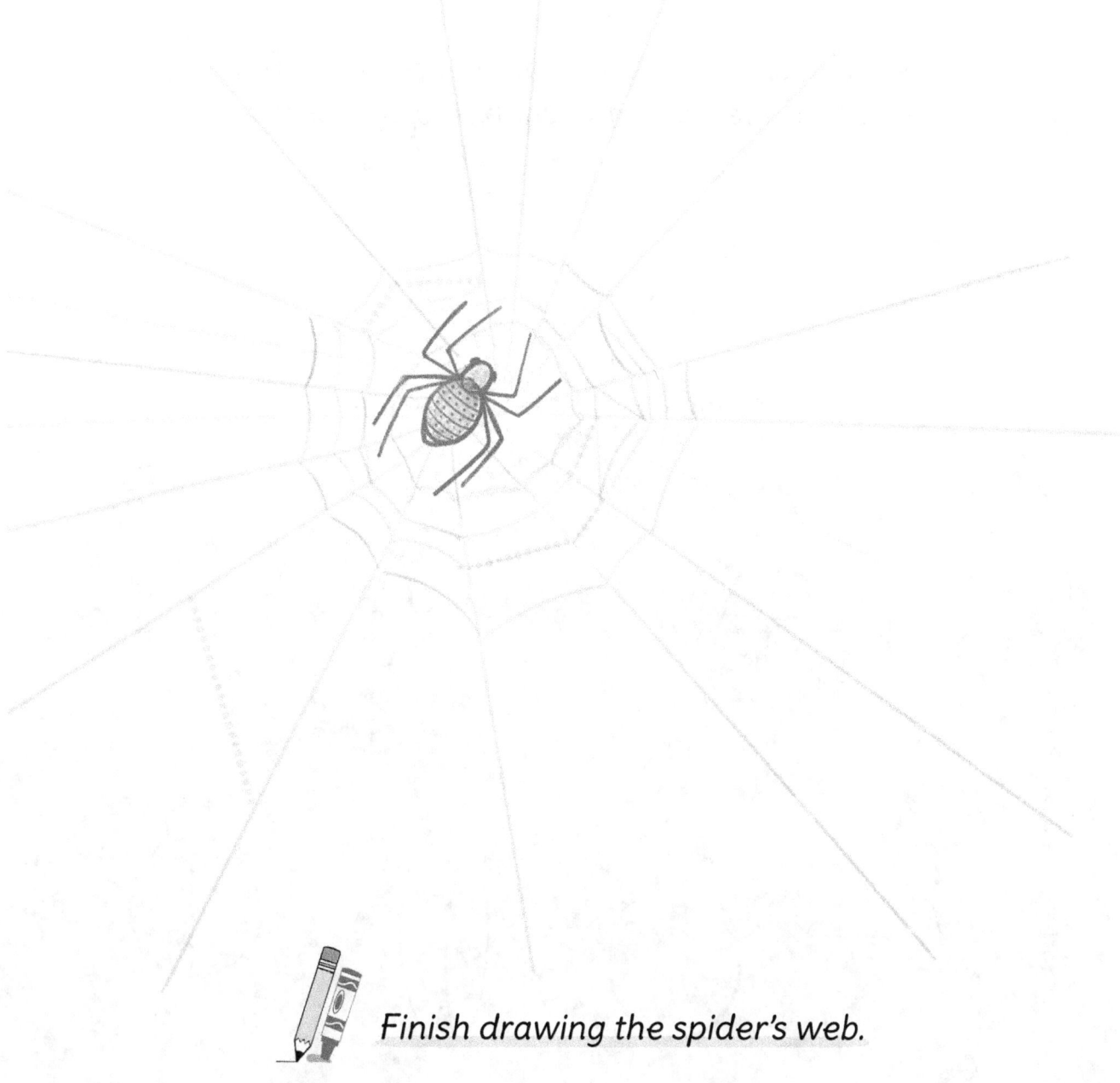

Finish drawing the spider's web.

Spiders are crawling creatures with eight legs that help them move, climb, and catch food. Along with scorpions, daddy longlegs, and mites, they belong to a group called arachnids. Most spiders have six or eight eyes, yet some still don't see well. Many spin webs using silk that comes from their bodies. Each web is unique and can look like triangles, wheels, or other shapes. These webs help spiders trap flies, mosquitoes, and moths. Can you believe some spiders eat their own webs?

BEETLE

Most insects, including ants, bees, beetles, butterflies, dragonflies, flies, and grasshoppers, have six legs.

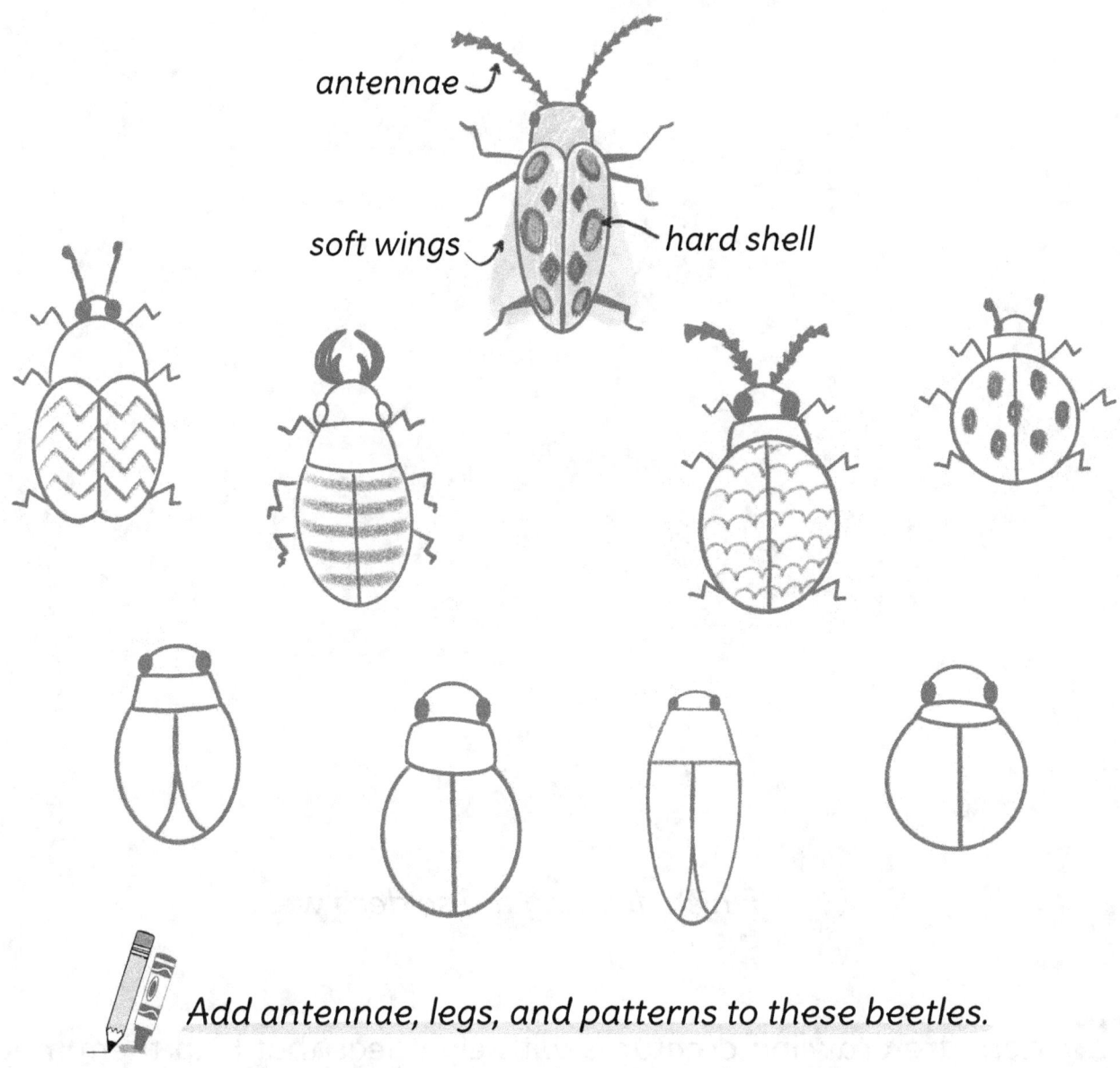

antennae

soft wings

hard shell

Add antennae, legs, and patterns to these beetles.

Beetles are insects that come in many shapes and bright colors. Some can glow in the dark like little lanterns. They have two antennae on their heads and two pairs of wings: a soft pair for flying and a tough pair that shields the softer wings. To warn and scare off predators, some beetles can make clicking or hissing noises.

 Animals by Alisa Bloom | Draw & Learn™ Book Series

BUTTERFLY

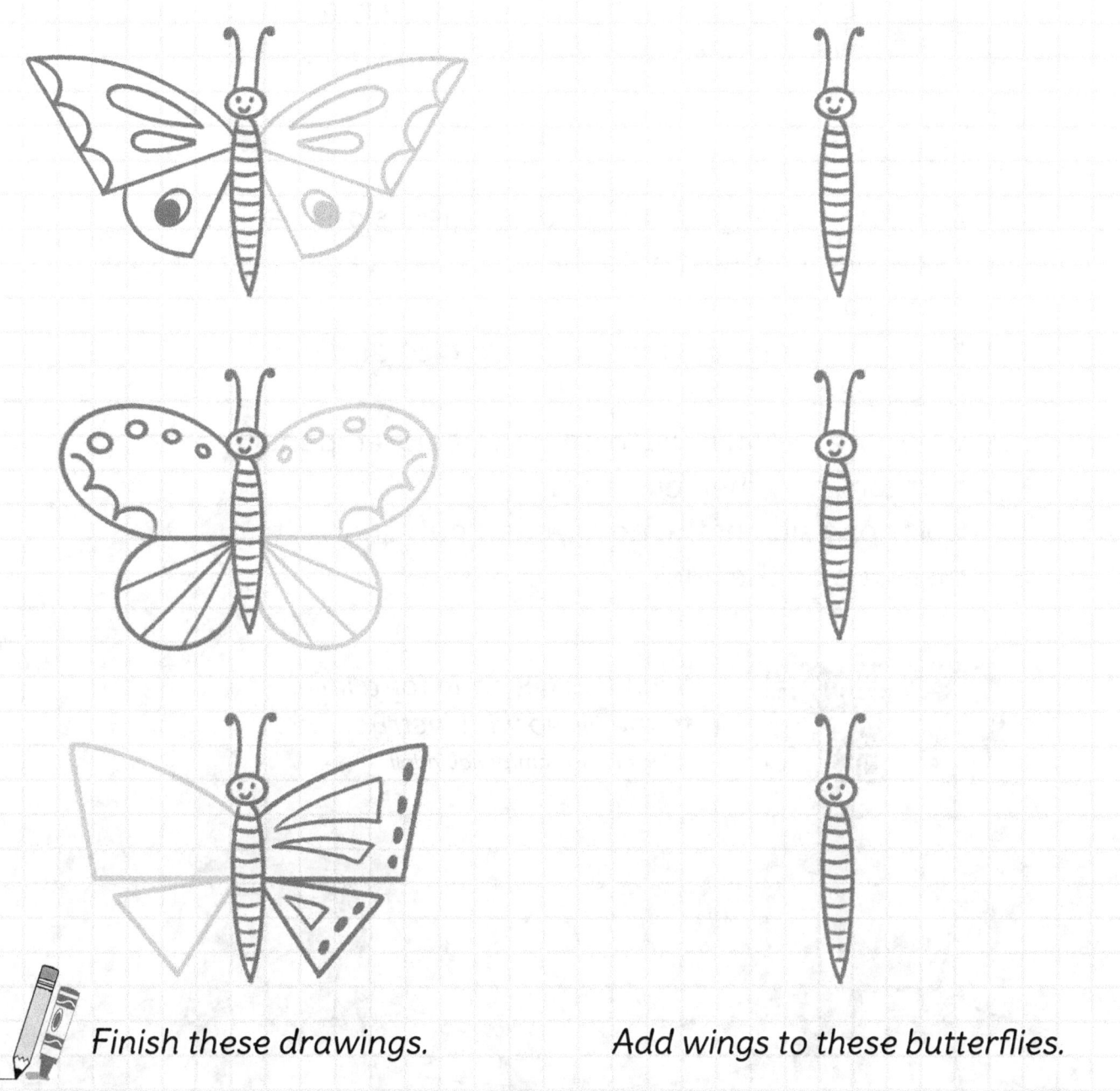

Finish these drawings.   *Add wings to these butterflies.*

Butterflies have pretty wings with colorful patterns. They spend their days flying around, basking in the warm sun, and sipping nectar — the sweet liquid from flowers. Baby butterflies hatch from tiny eggs and start their lives as **caterpillars** without wings. They eat plants and grow quickly before turning into beautiful butterflies. Isn't it amazing?

Make a Paper Doll

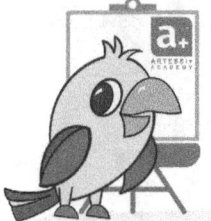

Great job, Artist! Now let's get ready for a fun craft project to put your creativity to work.

Instructions

- Cut out the penguin and heart patterns on the next page.
- Trace each pattern onto thicker paper, like cardstock or watercolor paper.
- Draw the penguin's face. You can also add a hat, scarf, or sweater.
- Color the penguin using crayons, colored pencils, or markers, and then cut it out.
- Color one side of the heart, cut it out, and write a message on the back.

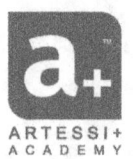  *Scan this QR code for a link to the video with instructions.*
video.artessi.com/penguindoll

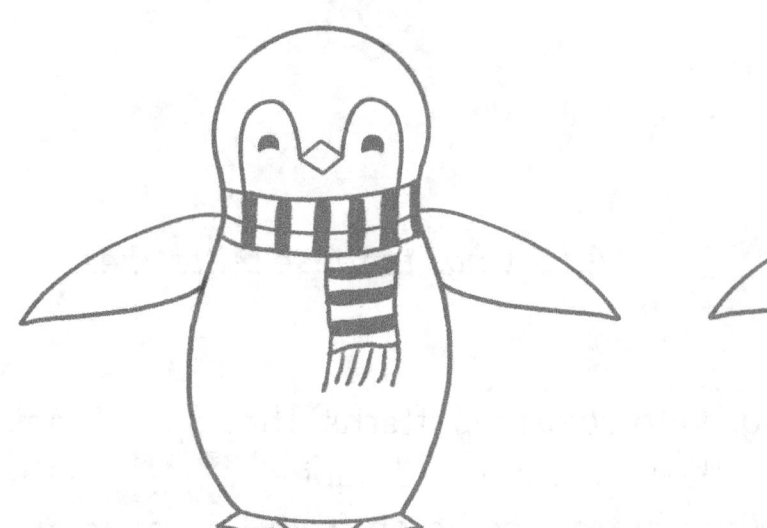

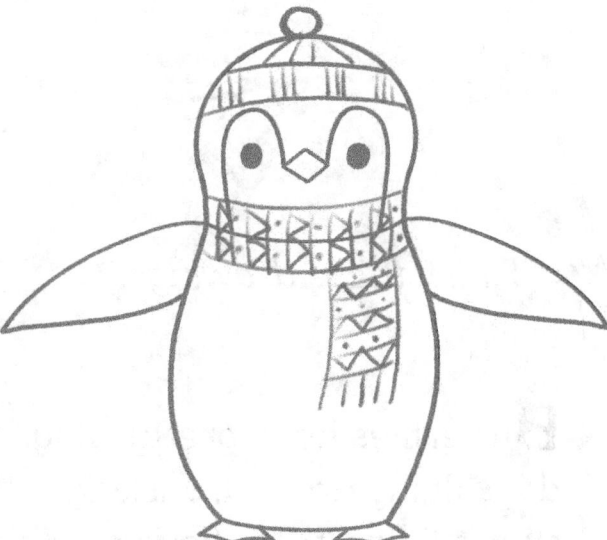

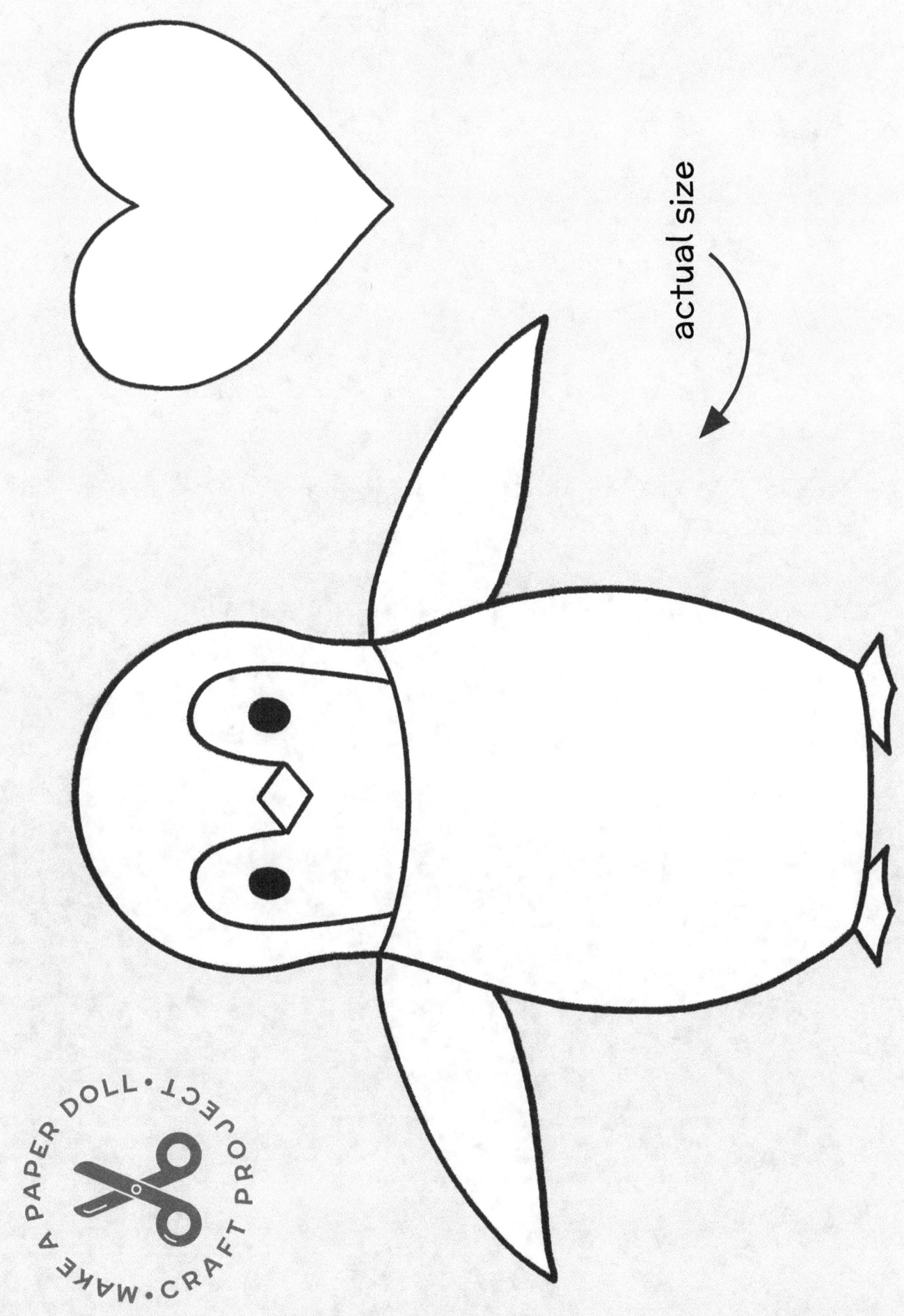

actual size

Draw & Learn™

Sketchbook

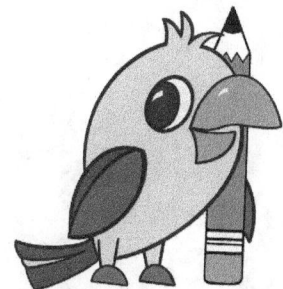

This **Draw & Learn™ Sketchbook** is a special place for you to draw and use your imagination. Let's turn your ideas into amazing drawings!

CREATIVE ART SPACE FOR CURIOUS KIDS

Discover Draw & Learn™ books, journals, and more at
www.artessi.com

? Questions

1

2

3

4

5

! Ideas

1

2

3

4

5

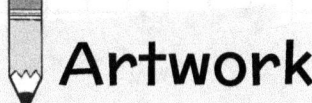
Artwork

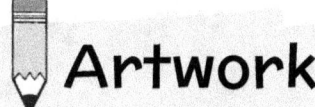
Artwork